*e*MoviePoster.com

presents

Vintage Hollywood Posters VII

Every item pictured in this book will be auctioned by **eMoviePoster.com** on the Internet from 7/1/04-7/11/04 (all items will close on 7/11 between 5 PM CST & 9 PM CST). Complete detailed descriptions of every item (including high quality digital images and detailed condition descriptions) can be found on our website **http://www.emovieposter.com**

IN THIS AUCTION THERE ARE:
NO Buyer's Premiums
NO U.S. Shipping Charges
NO Sales Tax (except in Missouri)
See our website for full details!

IMPORTANT NOTICE:
In addition to the aution of the items in this volume THERE WILL BE A REMARKABLE AUCTION OF JOHN WAYNE MOVIE POSTERS 6/30/04-7/10/04! Along with the items in this catalog, eMoviePoster.com will also auction an amazing collection of 334 movie posters, lobby cards and glass slides from EVERY western movie John Wayne ever made, including almost every one-sheet movie poster known to exist (original and re-release)! The collection was assembled over decades, but every item in it will be auctioned on July 10, 2004. The auction runs from June 30th to July 10th (see our website for full details).

Edited and Published by Bruce Hershenson
P.O. Box 874, West Plains, MO 65775
Phone: **(417) 256-9616** Fax: **(417) 257-6948**
mail@brucehershenson.com (e-mail)
http://**www.emovieposter.com** (website)

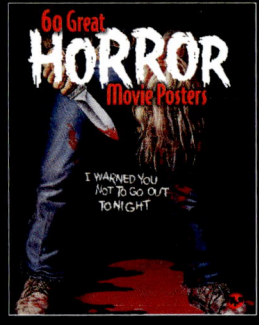 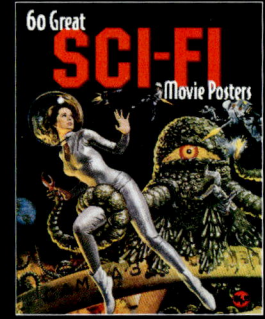 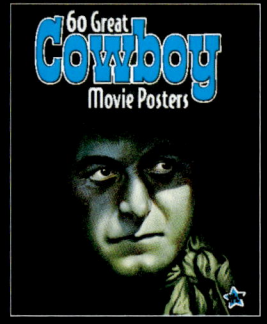 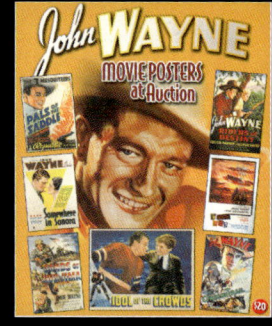

IF YOU ENJOYED THIS MOVIE POSTER BOOK, THEN YOU ARE SURE TO ENJOY THESE OTHER SIMILAR BRUCE HERSHENSON PUBLICATIONS. LOOK FOR THEM AT YOUR LOCAL BOOKSTORE OR ORDER THEM DIRECT FROM THE PUBLISHER.

 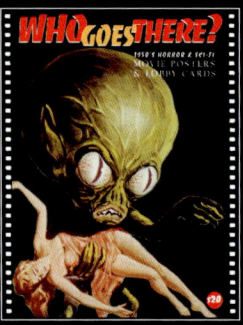 

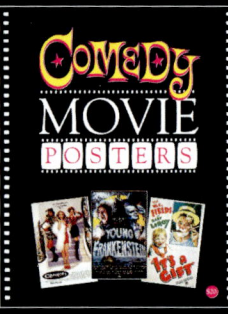 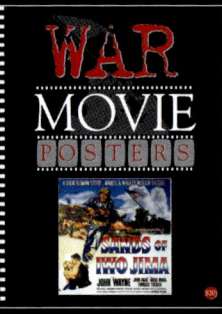 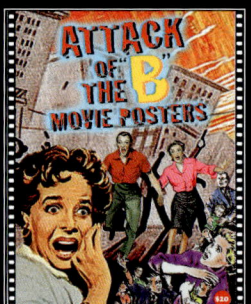 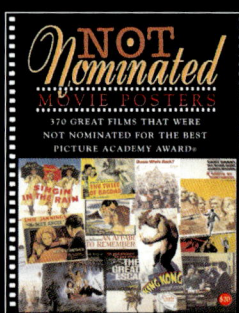

 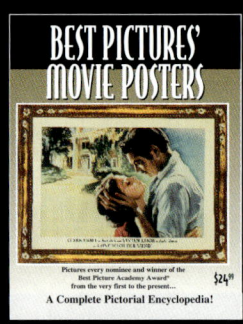 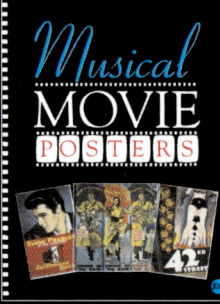  

 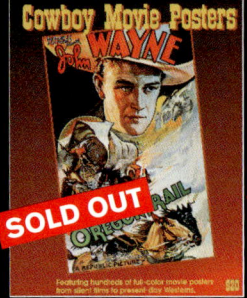  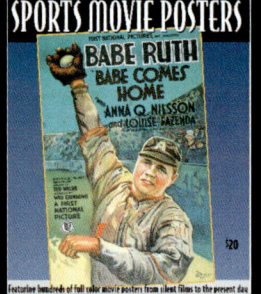  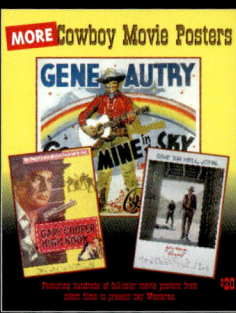

INTRODUCTION

My name is Bruce Hershenson and in 1990 I organized the very first all-movie poster auction ever held by a major auction house! It was a complete success, with all 271 lots selling for just under one million dollars. Since then I organized 12 more major "live" movie poster auctions (nine more for Christie's auction house and three for Howard Lowery auctions) with total sales of just under ten million dollars. In between, I sold over 30,000 movie posters and lobby cards through semi-annual sales catalogs with sales of over four million dollars.

In 1999 I opened eMoviePoster.com on the Internet, which has since become the most visited vintage movie poster website, with nearly 700,000 visitors to date. In mid-2000 I started weekly Tuesday night auctions on the eBay auction site, and in over 200 nearly consecutive weekly auctions to date have auctioned more than 135,000 items, with total sales of over SEVEN million dollars!

I published an elaborate full-color auction catalog for each major auction I organized (just like what you are holding in your hands), and in addition have published 22 reference volumes to movie posters, for a total of 38 volumes to date, which combined have sold more than 300,000 copies!

In 2001 I decided to move my major auctions to the Internet. On June 30 and July 1, 2001 (in Vintage Hollywood Posters IV), I auctioned 711 items for a total of $717,000. Those who have purchased items at other major auctions are all too familiar with the many added fees tacked on after the auction's close, including a buyer,s premium that ranges from 15% to 20%, and shipping fees that range from high to outrageous. But in THIS auction, Vintage Hollywood Posters IV, there were NO Buyer's Premiums, NO U.S. Shipping charges, and NO Sales Tax (except in Missouri). This saved most buyers from 30% to 40%!

I also provided complete detailed descriptions of every item. Many major auctions only provide bidders with fuzzy images and fuzzier condition descriptions, glossing over condition defects and restoration. I provided high quality digital images, and detailed condition descriptions (including detailed descriptions of each restored item's PRE-restoration condition, something NO other major auction house provides). In 2002 and 2003 I repeated the process with Vintage Hollywood Posters V & VI, with combined sales of just over one million dollars!

NOW I PRESENT MY FOURTH MAJOR ONLINE AUCTION, VINTAGE HOLLYWOOD POSTERS VII (which is being held in conjunction with a special auction of John Wayne movie posters; see below for further information). The Vintage Hollywood Posters VII auction will end on 7/11/04 (there will be preliminary bidding from July 1-11).

ONCE AGAIN, THERE ARE NO BUYER'S PREMIUMS, NO U.S. SHIPPING CHARGES AND NO SALES TAX (except in Missouri), which will again save buyers 30% to 40%! Also, note that in Vintage Hollywood Posters VII, you will find many items that are financially well within the reach of ANY collector. But I did not sacrifice quality to include these more reasonably priced items. I carefully sought out the most desired posters, lobby cards and glass slides from the most collected films, the kind of items that most collectors are actively seeking, but have great difficulty finding, especially in top condition.

IMPORTANT NOTICE: THERE WILL ALSO BE A REMARKABLE AUCTION OF JOHN WAYNE MOVIE POSTERS 6/30/04-7/10/04! Along with the items in this catalog, eMoviePoster.com will auction an amazing collection of 334 movie posters, lobby cards and glass slides from EVERY western movie John Wayne ever made, including almost every one-sheet movie poster known to exist (original and re-release)! The collection was assembled over decades, but every item in it will be auctioned on July 10, 2004. The auction runs from June 30th to July 10th (see our website for full details).

AN IMPORTANT ANNOUNCEMENT REGARDING THE POSTERS AND LOBBY CARDS IN THIS VOLUME!

All of the items pictured in this book will be auctioned by eMoviePoster.com on the Internet on 7/11/04. If you are reading this PRIOR to that date, go to http://www.emovieposter.com to find out how to bid (if you don't have Internet access, call 417 256 9616 and we'll make arrangements for you to bid another way). If you are reading this AFTER 7/11/04, you will find a sheet added to this volume that gives the prices every item sold for. If you have items you would like us to consider for our future auctions, go to http://www.emovieposter.com/consign.htm and read our terms, or, if you don't have Internet access, call us or mail us a list of your posters (see the first page of this book for full contact info). If you are interested in buying movie posters or lobby cards, or in learning more about the hobby, you should visit our website at http://www.emovieposter.com, where you will find thousands of images of the very best movie posters, as well as lots of information important to every collector.

PLEASE NOTE THAT ALL OF THE POSTERS IN THIS VOLUME ARE THE ORIGINAL RELEASE ONE-SHEET (27" X 41") MOVIE POSTER, UNLESS OTHERWISE NOTED.

You can find out all you need to know about bidding on items in this most exciting auction by going to my website, http://www.emovieposter.com where you can also view this entire catalog in an online digital format.

Phillip Wages (who created my online auctions and also much of my website) and Amy Knight (who did the layouts and cover design for this book and many of my previous books) gave considerable assistance in the preparation of this auction and this catalog, and I thank them very much.

Bruce Hershenson
June 2004

1. WAR EXPOSITION, 1918

2. EAST IS WEST, 1922

3. THE TRAIL OF THE LONESOME PINE, 1923

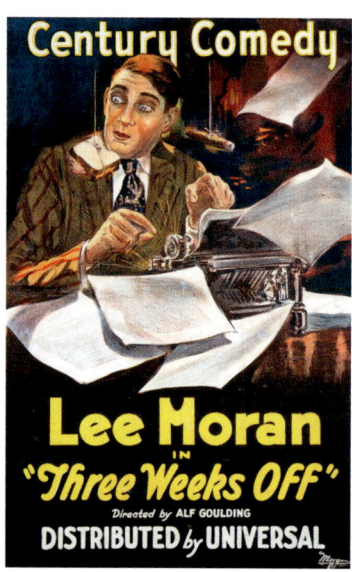
4. THREE WEEKS OFF, 1922

5. MINNIE, 1922

6. THE BATTLESHIP POTEMKIN, 1925, 1st Japanese release, 1967

7. UN CHIEN ANDALOU, 1929, 1st French release, 1968

8. FEET FIRST, 1930

9. THE GOLD RUSH, 1925, lobby card

10. THE GOLD RUSH, 1925, lobby card

11. STOCKS AND BLONDES, 1928

12. THE LONE RIDER, 1930

13. DUCK SOUP, 1933, lobby card

14. MONKEY BUSINESS, 1931, window card

15. LAUREL AND HARDY, 1932, personality poster

16. CHARLIE CHAN IN PARIS, 1935, Australian daybill

17. CHARLIE CHAN AT THE WAX MUSEUM, 1940, Australian daybill

19. THE SCARLET EMPRESS, 1934, window card

18. CHARLIE CHAN IN SHANGHAI, 1935, Italian one-sheet

20. THE DEVIL IS A WOMAN, 1935, window card

21. ROSE MARIE, 1936

22-29. ROSE MARIE, 1936, lobby cards

30. BOLERO, 1934, lobby card

31. HERE COMES THE NAVY, 1934, French

32. BAR 20 JUSTICE, 1938

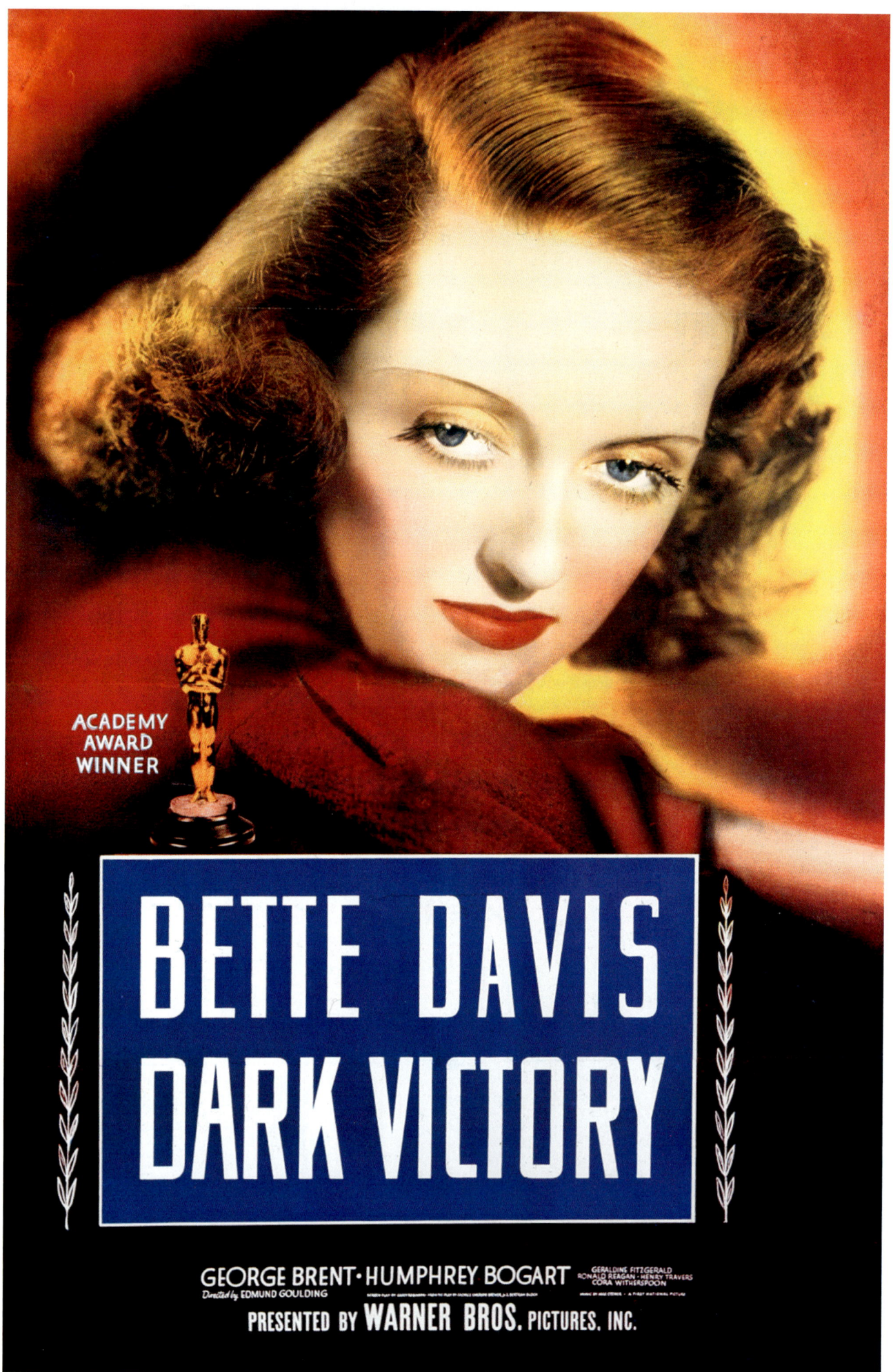

33. DARK VICTORY, 1939

34. THEY LEARNED ABOUT WOMEN, 1930

35. A DAMSEL IN DISTRESS, 1937

36. MEN IN WHITE, 1934, Belgian

37. BLUEBEARD'S 8th WIFE, 1938

38. TARZAN FINDS A SON, 1939

39. LITTLE MISS MARKER, 1934, insert

40. KING OF BURLESQUE, 1935

41. ZIEGFELD FOLLIES, 1945, insert

42. EAST IS WEST, 1930, six-sheet

43. PARDON MY SARONG, 1942, French, one-panel

44. MR BLANDINGS BUILDS HIS DREAM HOUSE, 1948, three-sheet

45. JEW SUSS, 1934, Belgian

46. THE WHITE COCKATOO, 1935

47. THE SEA HAWK, 1940, window card

48. ANNIE OAKLEY, 1935, half-sheet

49. MARIHUANA, 1935, 1940s reissue lobby card

50. TOBACCO ROAD, 1941, half-sheet

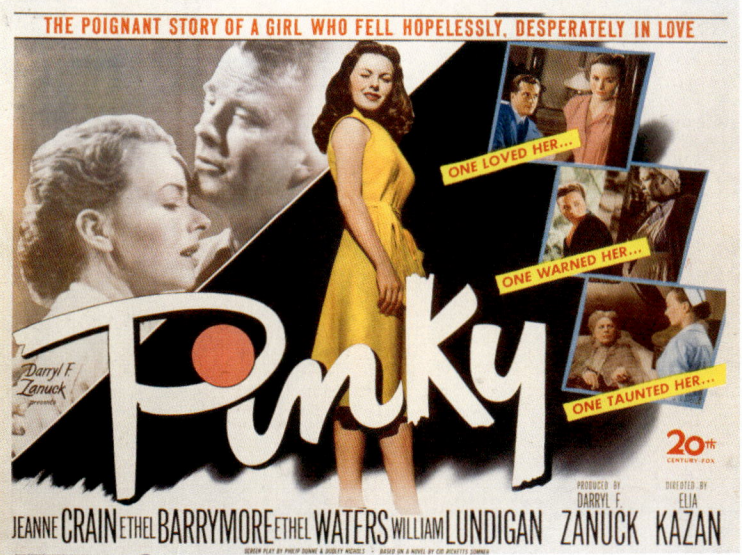
51. PINKY, 1949, half-sheet

52. PINOCCHIO, 1940, insert

53. GULLIVER'S TRAVELS, 1939

54. ANOTHER NEW POPEYE COMEDY, 1934

55. CASABLANCA, 1942, lobby card

56. CASABLANCA, 1942, 1956 reissue half-sheet

57. CASABLANCA, 1942, Japanese, 1974 reissue

58. THE GAY FALCON, 1941

59. SHERLOCK HOLMES FACES DEATH, 1943

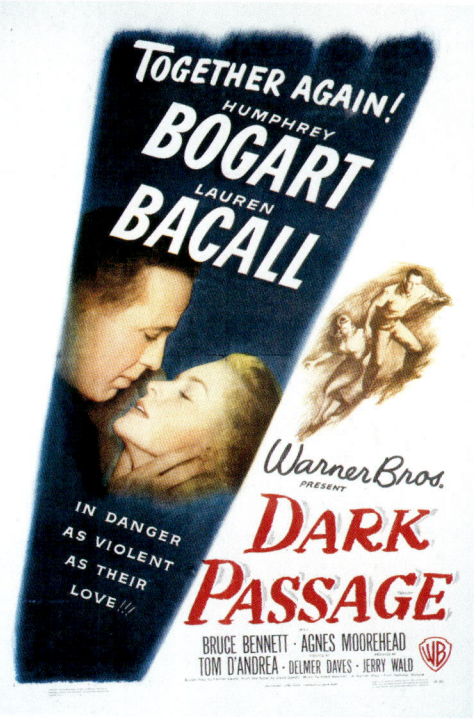
60. DARK PASSAGE, 1947

61. OUT OF THE PAST, 1947, lobby card, autographed by Robert Mitchum and Jane Greer

62. DOUBLE INDEMNITY, 1944, lobby card

63. SABOTEUR, 1942, Argentinean

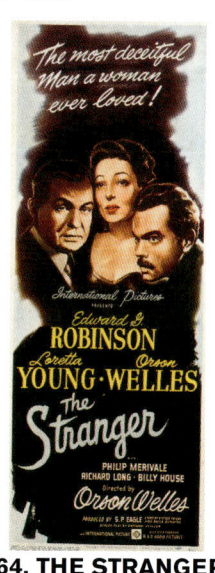
64. THE STRANGER, 1946, insert

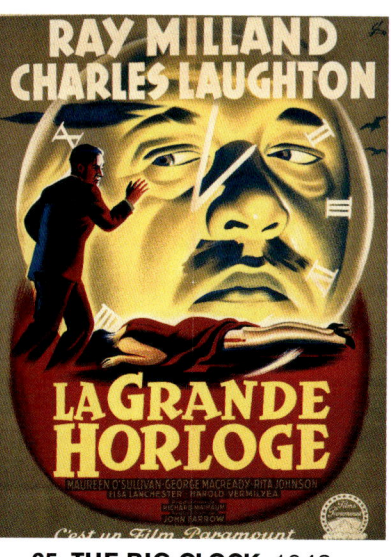
65. THE BIG CLOCK, 1948, French 23x32

66. THE 3rd MAN, 1949, 1950s reissue

67. BEAUTY AND THE BEAST, 1946, medium French

68. BEAUTY AND THE BEAST, 1946, Belgian

69. 20,000 LEAGUES UNDER THE SEA, 1955, Thirty by Forty

70. THE SEVENTH VOYAGE OF SINBAD, 1958, Italian, two-panel

71. FROM THE EARTH TO THE MOON, 1958

72-79. FLASH GORDON, 1936, lobby cards (serial version, Chapter 5)

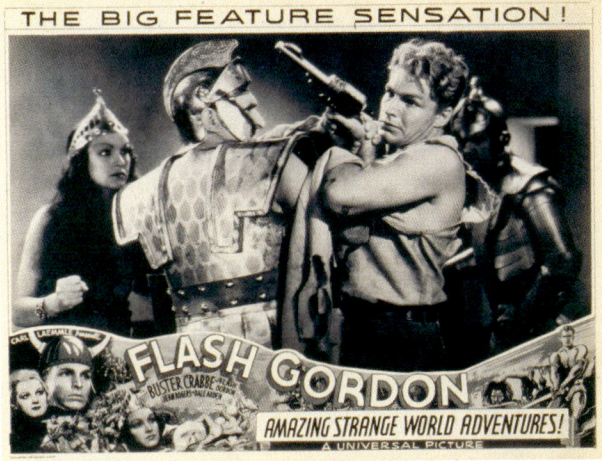
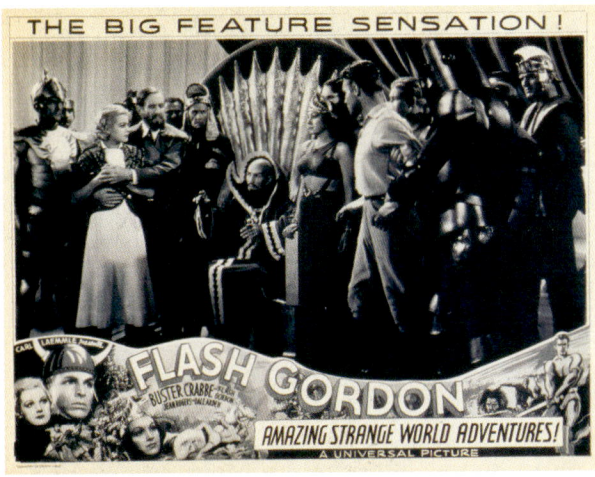

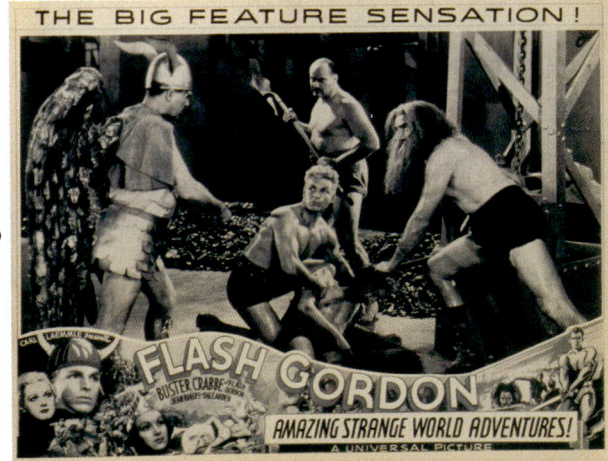

80-87. FLASH GORDON, 1936, lobby cards (feature version)

88. FRANKENSTEIN MEETS THE WOLF MAN, 1943

89. DRACULA, 1931, title card, 1938 reissue

90. THE RETURN OF THE VAMPIRE, 1944, half-sheet

91. SON OF FRANKENSTEIN, 1939, 1953 reissue, half-sheet

92. THE BRIDE OF FRANKENSTEIN, 1935, 1953 reissue title lobby card

93. JUGGERNAUT, 1936

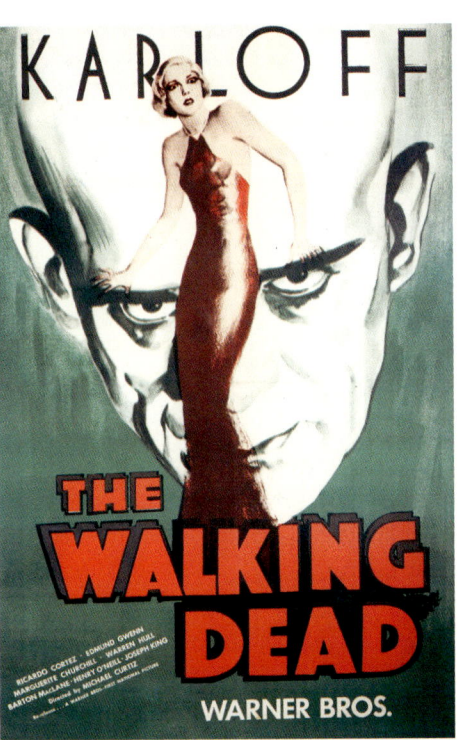

94. THE WALKING DEAD, 1936, 1940s reissue

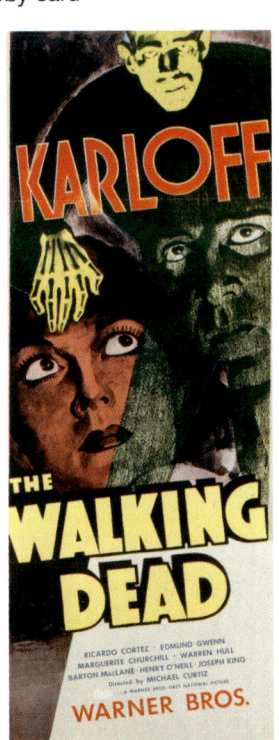

95. THE WALKING DEAD, 1936, 1940s reissue, insert

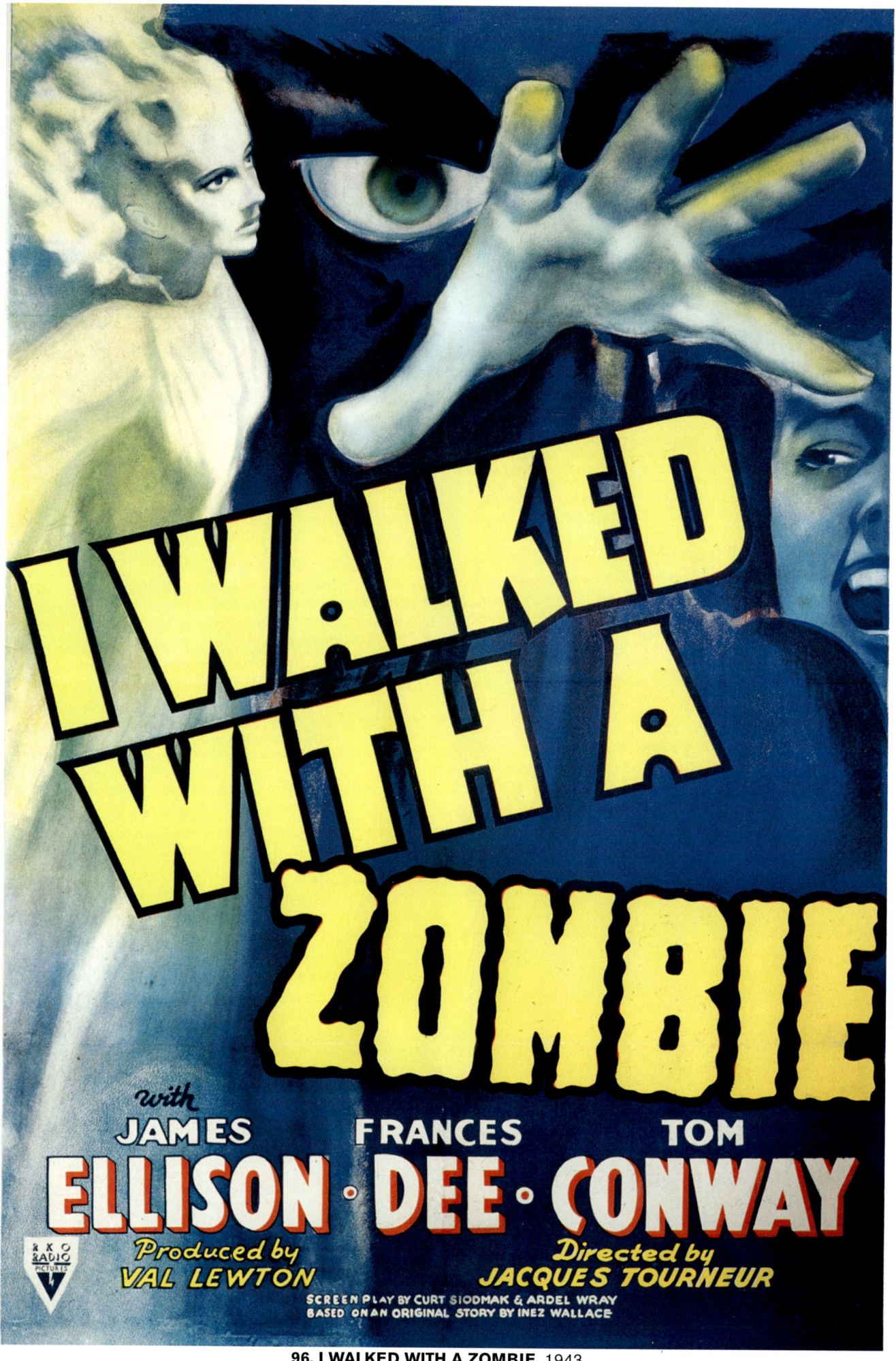

96. I WALKED WITH A ZOMBIE, 1943

97. ABBOTT AND COSTELLO MEET FRANKENSTEIN, 1948, window card

98. HOLD THAT GHOST, 1941, window card

99. ABBOTT AND COSTELLO MEET FRANKENSTEIN, 1948, Belgian

100. ABBOTT AND COSTELLO GO TO MARS, 1953

101. FRANKENSTEIN, 1931, glass slide, (first style)

102. FRANKENSTEIN, 1931, glass slide, (second style)

103. DRACULA, 1931, glass slide

104. THE MUMMY, 1932, glass slide

105. THE UNHOLY THREE, 1925, glass slide

107. SVENGALI, 1931, glass slide

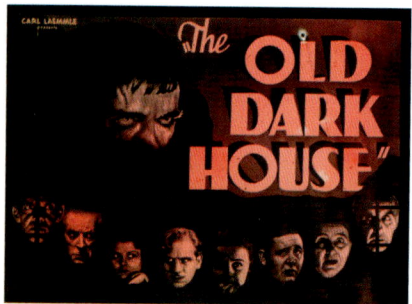
109. THE OLD DARK HOUSE, 1932, glass slide

106. LONDON AFTER MIDNIGHT, 1927, glass slide

108. MURDERS IN THE RUE MORGUE, 1932, glass slide

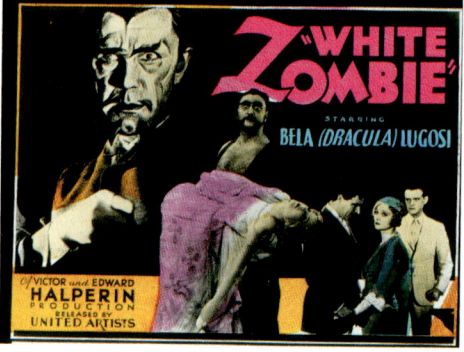
110. WHITE ZOMBIE, 1932, glass slide

111. KING KONG, 1933, glass slide

112. THE BLACK CAT, 1934, glass slide

113. THE BRIDE OF FRANKENSTEIN, 1935, glass slide

114. THE INVISIBLE RAY, 1936, glass slide

115. THE MYSTERY OF MR WONG, 1938, glass slide

116. TOWER OF LONDON, 1939, glass slide

117. SON OF FRANKENSTEIN, 1939, glass slide

118. MR WONG IN CHINATOWN, 1939, glass slide

119. THE FATAL HOUR, 1940, glass slide

120. BLACK FRIDAY, 1940, glass slide

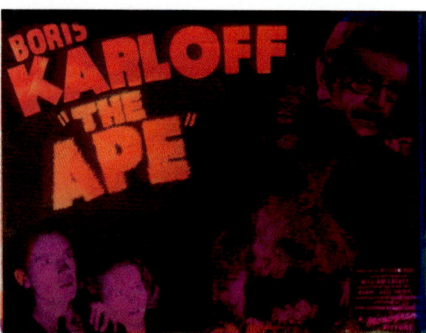
121. THE APE, 1940, glass slide

122. THE BLACK CAT, 1941, glass slide

123. INVISIBLE GHOST, 1941, glass slide

124. BRIGHT EYES, 1934, glass slide

125. THE LITTLEST REBEL, 1935, glass slide

126. THE LITTLE COLONEL, 1935, glass slide

127. CURLY TOP, 1935, glass slide

128. THE POOR LITTLE RICH GIRL, 1936, glass slide

129. CAPTAIN JANUARY, 1936, glass slide

130. HEIDI, 1937, glass slide

131. CLEOPATRA, 1917, glass slide

132. SUNNYSIDE, 1919, glass slide

133. A ROMANCE OF HAPPY VALLEY, 1919, glass slide

134. LOVES OF PHARAOH, 1922, glass slide

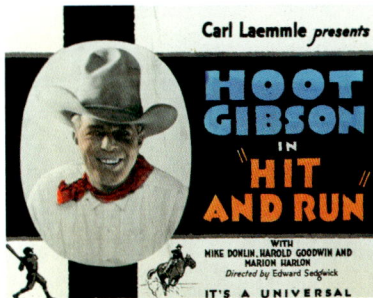
135. HIT AND RUN, 1924, glass slide

136. OH YOU TONY, 1924, glass slide

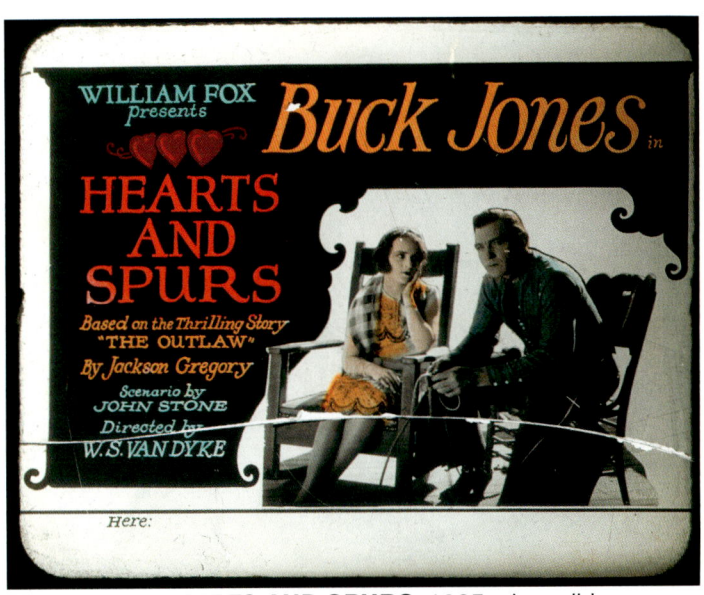
137. HEARTS AND SPURS, 1925, glass slide

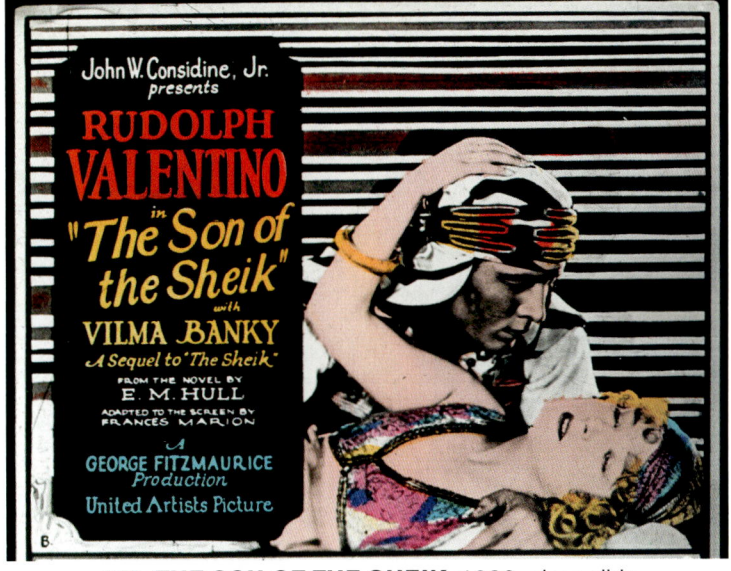
138. THE SON OF THE SHEIK, 1926, glass slide

139. SPARROWS, 1926, glass slide

140. THE CROWD, 1928, glass slide

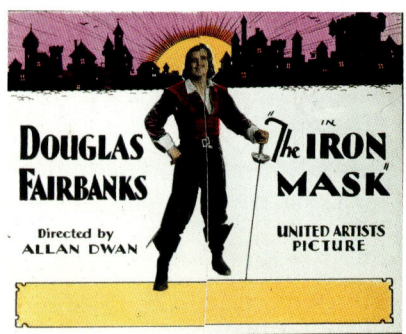
141. THE IRON MASK, 1929, glass slide

142. SEVEN DAYS' LEAVE, 1930, glass slide

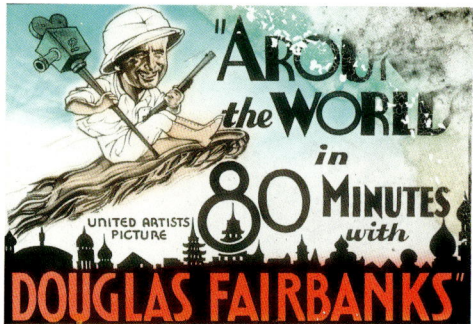
143. AROUND THE WORLD IN 80 \MINUTES, 1931, glass slide

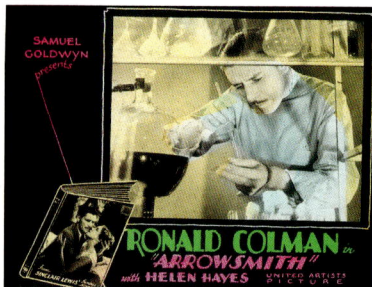
144. ARROWSMITH, 1931, glass slide

145. HONOR OF THE FAMILY, 1931, glass slide

146. ILLICIT, 1931, glass slide

147. INSPIRATION, 1931, glass slide

148. KIKI, 1931, glass slide

149. MATA HARI, 1931, glass slide

150. SUSAN LENOX, 1931, glass slide

151. THE GENERAL, 1927, glass slide

152. PARLOR BEDROOM AND BATH, 1931, glass slide

153. SIDEWALKS OF NEW YORK, 1931, glass slide

154. CITY LIGHTS, 1931, glass slide

155. MODERN TIMES, 1936, glass slide

156. YOU CAN'T CHEAT AN HONEST MAN, 1939, glass slide

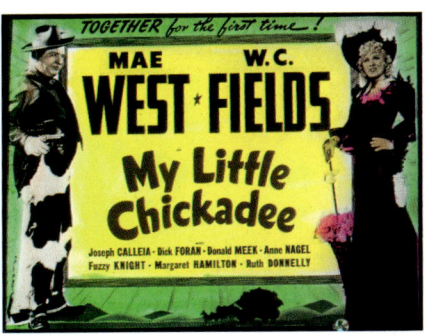
157. MY LITTLE CHICKADEE, 1940, glass slide

158. THE GREAT DICTATOR, 1940, glass slide

159. DAVID COPPERFIELD, 1935, glass slide

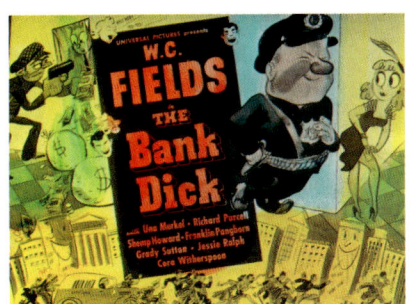
160. THE BANK DICK, 1940, glass slide

161. THE COCOANUTS, 1929, glass slide

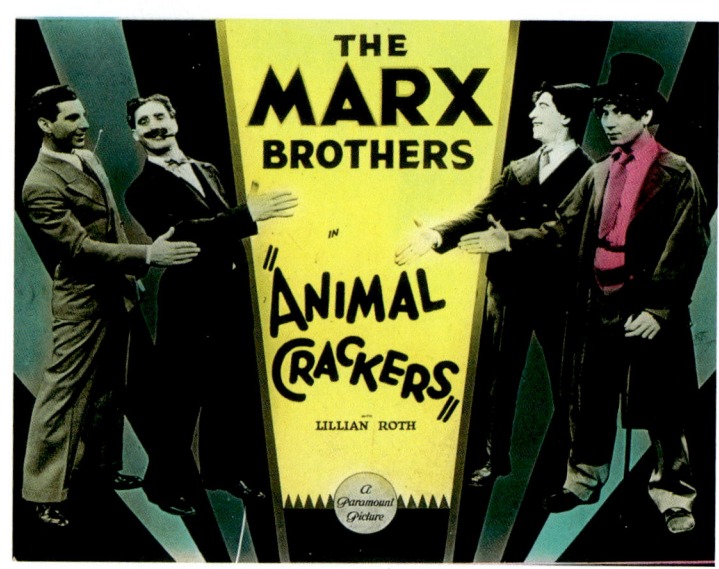

162. ANIMAL CRACKERS, 1930, glass slide

163. HORSE FEATHERS, 1932, glass slide

164. A DAY AT THE RACES, 1937, glass slide

165. ROOM SERVICE, 1938, glass slide

166. AT THE CIRCUS, 1939, glass slide

167. GO WEST, 1940, glass slide

168. THE BIG STORE, 1941, glass slide

169. BUCK PRIVATES, 1940, glass slide

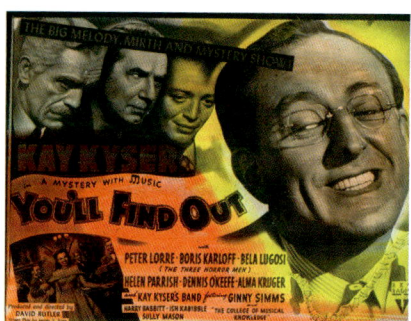

170. YOU'LL FIND OUT, 1940, glass slide

171. PARDON US, 1931, glass slide

172. SONS OF THE DESERT, 1933, glass slide

173. WAY OUT WEST, 1937, glass slide

174. PICK A STAR, 1937, glass slide

175. BLOCK-HEADS, 1938, glass slide

176. SWISS MISS, 1938, glass slide

177. THE FLYING DEUCES, 1939, glass slide

178. SAPS AT SEA, 1940, glass slide

179. A CHUMP AT OXFORD, 1940, glass slide

180. THE BULLFIGHTERS, 1945, glass slide

181. CHARLIE CHAN CARRIES ON, 1931, glass slide

182. THE BLACK CAMEL, 1931, glass slide

183. CHARLIE CHAN'S GREATEST CASE, 1933, glass slide

184. CHARLIE CHAN IN EGYPT, 1935, glass slide

185. CHARLIE CHAN IN LONDON, 1934, glass slide

186. CHARLIE CHAN IN SHANGHAI, 1935, glass slide

187. CHARLIE CHAN IN PARIS, 1935, glass slide

188. CHARLIE CHAN AT THE RACE TRACK, 1936, glass slide

189. CHARLIE CHAN AT THE OPERA, 1936, glass slide

190. CHARLIE CHAN ON BROADWAY, 1937, glass slide

191. CHARLIE CHAN AT MONTE CARLO, 1937, glass slide

192. CHARLIE CHAN AT THE OLYMPICS, 1937, glass slide

193. CHARLIE CHAN IN HONOLULU, 1938, glass slide

194. CHARLIE CHAN IN RENO, 1939, glass slide

195. A DAMSEL IN DISTRESS, 1937, glass slide

196. THE STORY OF VERNON AND IRENE CASTLE, 1939, glass slide

197. THE GAY DIVORCEE, 1934, glass slide

198. SWING TIME, 1936, glass slide

199. SHALL WE DANCE, 1937, glass slide

200. CAREFREE, 1938, glass slide

201. THE WIZARD OF OZ, 1939, glass slide

202. SNOW WHITE AND THE SEVEN DWARFS, 1938, glass slide, (first version)

203. PINOCCHIO, 1940, glass slide

204. SNOW WHITE AND THE SEVEN DWARFS, 1938, glass slide, (second version)

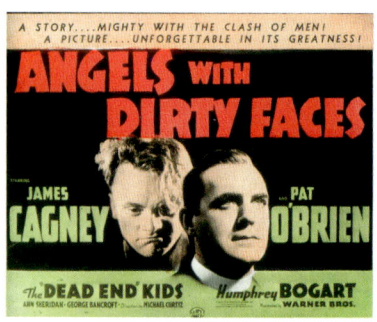
205. ANGELS WITH DIRTY FACES, 1938, glass slide

206. EACH DAWN I DIE, 1939, glass slide

207. THE ROARING TWENTIES, 1939, glass slide

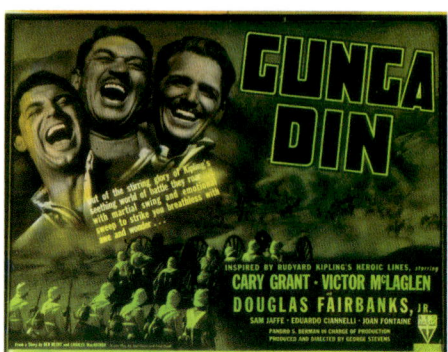
208. GUNGA DIN, 1939, glass slide

209. FOUR'S A CROWD, 1938, glass slide

210. TEST PILOT, 1938, glass slide

211. IT HAPPENED ONE NIGHT, 1934, glass slide

212. WUTHERING HEIGHTS, 1939, glass slide

213. LITTLE NELLIE KELLY, 1940, glass slide

214. TOO HOT TO HANDLE, 1938, glass slide

215. STRANGE CARGO, 1940, glass slide

216. LITTLE WOMEN, 1933, glass slide

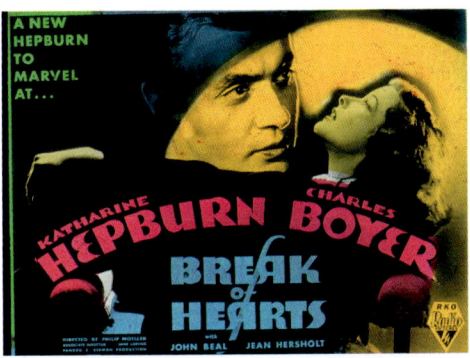
217. BREAK OF HEARTS, 1935, glass slide

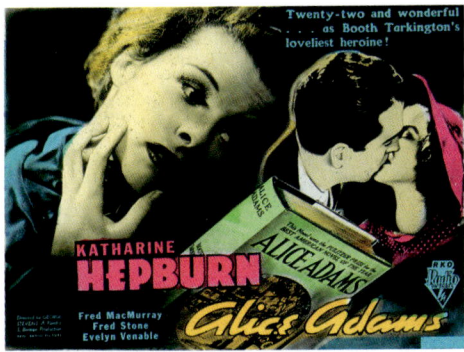
218. ALICE ADAMS, 1935, glass slide

219. BRINGING UP BABY, 1938, glass slide

220. THE PHILADELPHIA STORY, 1940, glass slide

221. FOOTLIGHT PARADE, 1933, glass slide

222. MY MAN GODFREY, 1936, glass slide

223. HELL'S ANGELS, 1930, glass slide

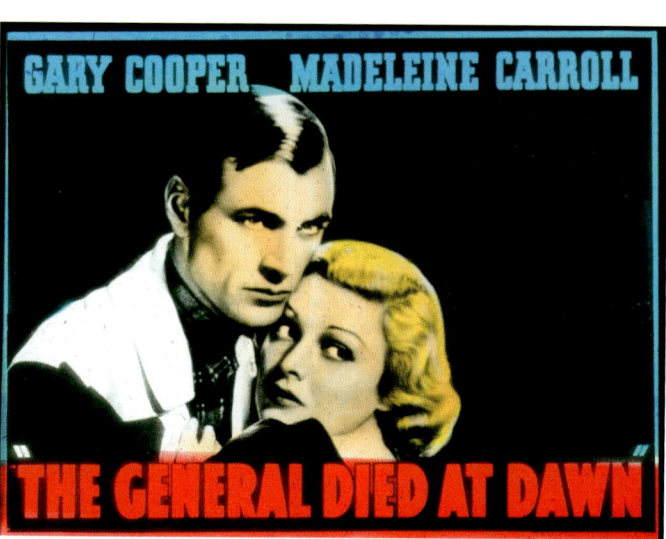
224. THE GENERAL DIED AT DAWN, 1936, glass slide

225. HELL DIVERS, 1932, glass slide

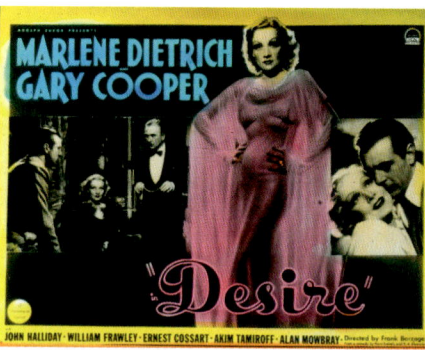
226. DESIRE, 1936, glass slide

227. LOVE ON THE RUN, 1936, glass slide

228. THREE WISE GIRLS, 1932, glass slide

229. THE WORKING MAN, 1933, glass slide

230. FOG OVER FRISCO, 1934, glass slide

231. THE HOUND OF THE BASKERVILLES, 1939, glass slide

232. REBECCA, 1940, glass slide

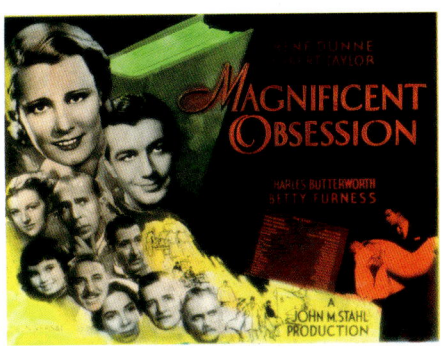

233. MAGNIFICENT OBSESSION, 1935, glass slide

234. SECOND CHORUS, 1940, glass slide

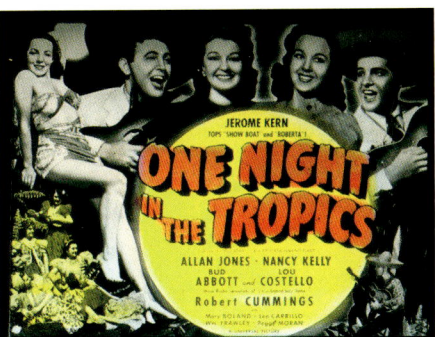

235. ONE NIGHT IN THE TROPICS, 1940, glass slide

236. CARELESS LADY, 1932, glass slide

237. THE HATCHET MAN, 1932, glass slide

238. EVELYN PRENTICE, 1934, glass slide

239. THE CROWD ROARS, 1932, glass slide

240. HALLELUJAH, I'M A BUM, 1933, glass slide

241. DESTINATION MOON, 1950, pressbook

242. CAT-WOMEN OF THE MOON, 1953

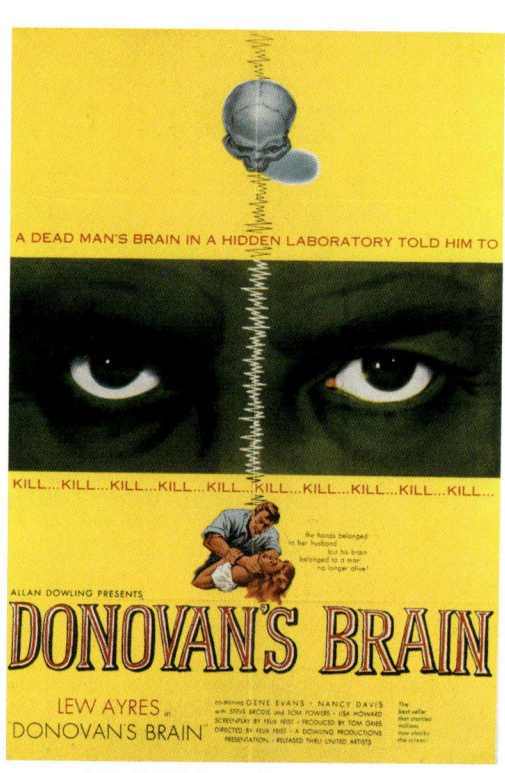

243. DONOVAN'S BRAIN, 1953

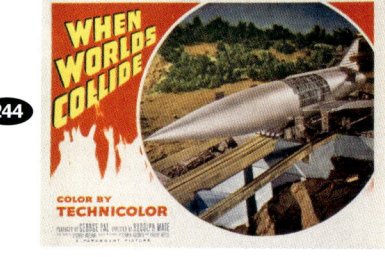

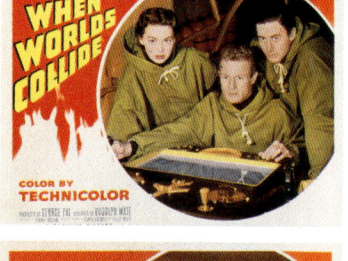

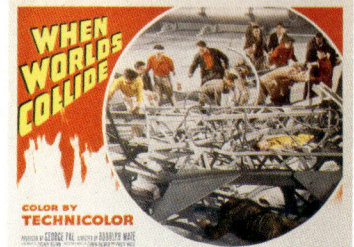
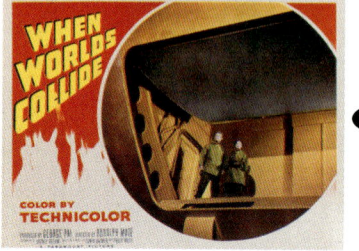

244-251. WHEN WORLDS COLLIDE, 1951, lobby cards

252. THE MAN FROM PLANET X, 1951

253. THE DAY THE EARTH STOOD STILL, 1951, window card

 254.
 255.
 256.
 257.
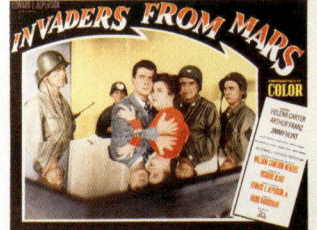 258.
 259.
 260.
 261.

254-261. INVADERS FROM MARS, 1953, lobby cards

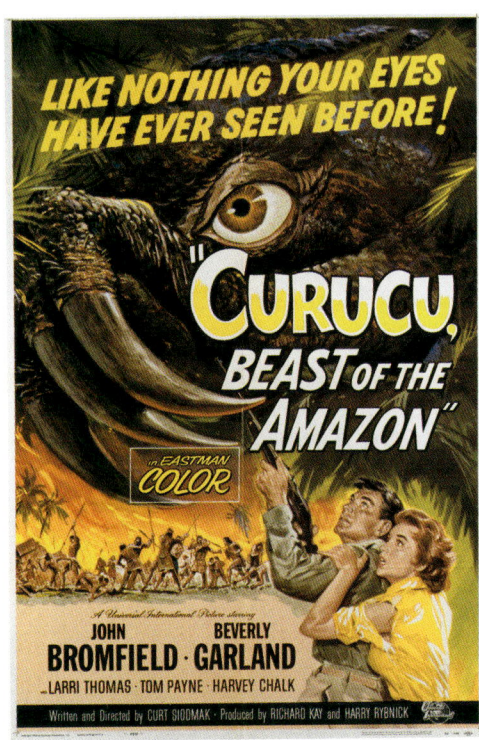

262. CURUCU, BEAST OF THE AMAZON, 1956

263. INVADERS FROM MARS, 1953, fantasy lobby card #9

264 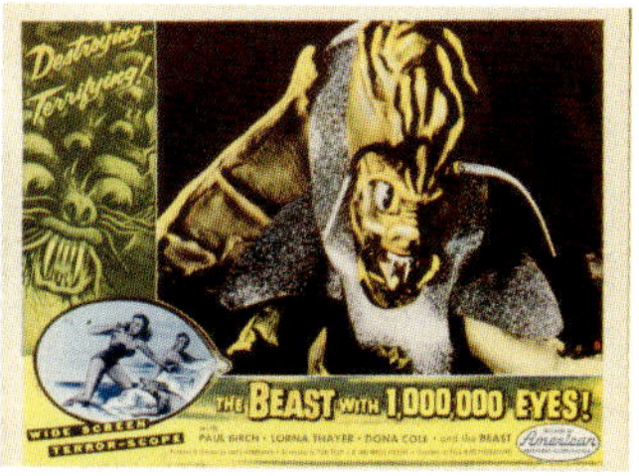

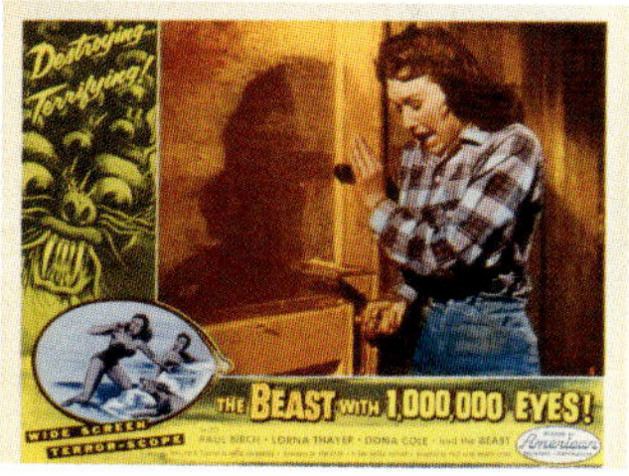 265

266 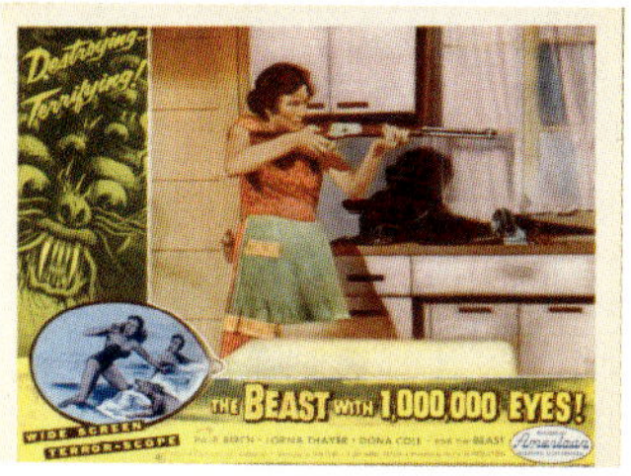

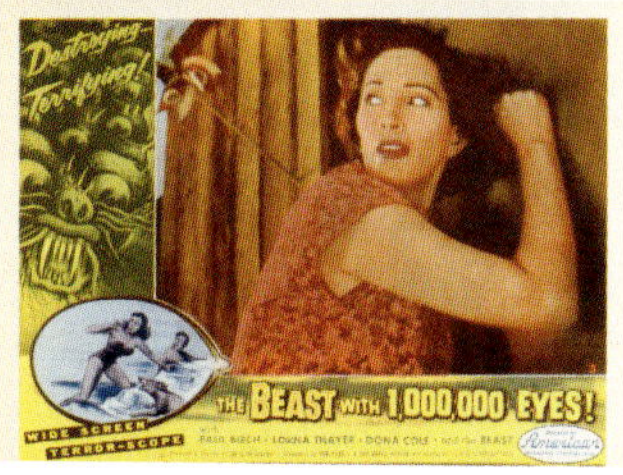 267

268 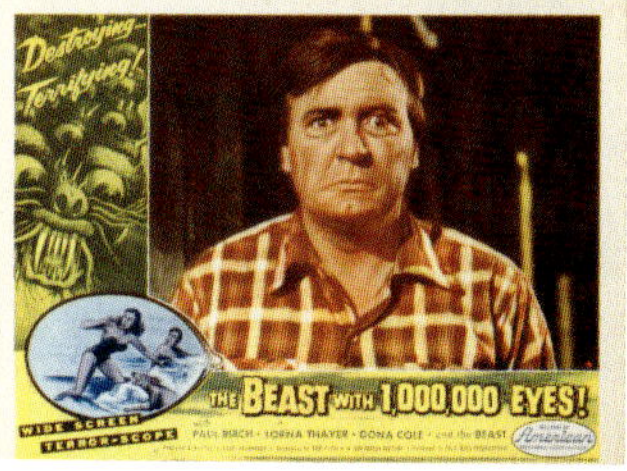

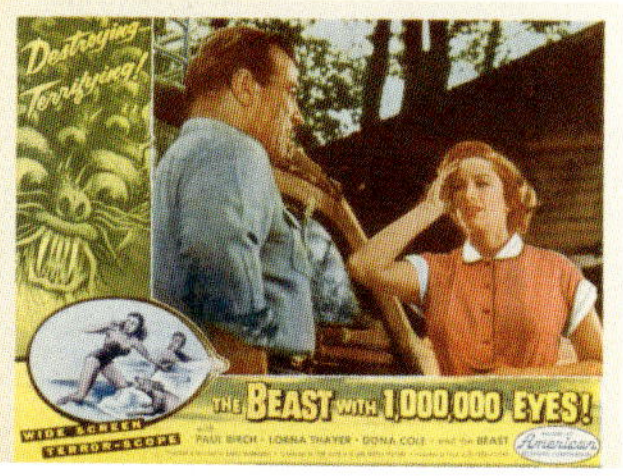 269

260 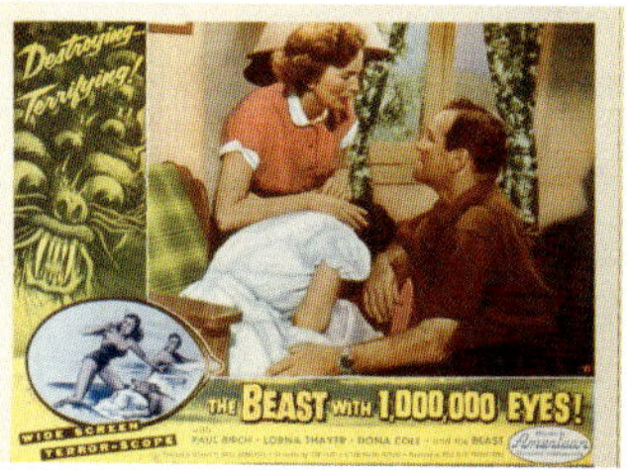

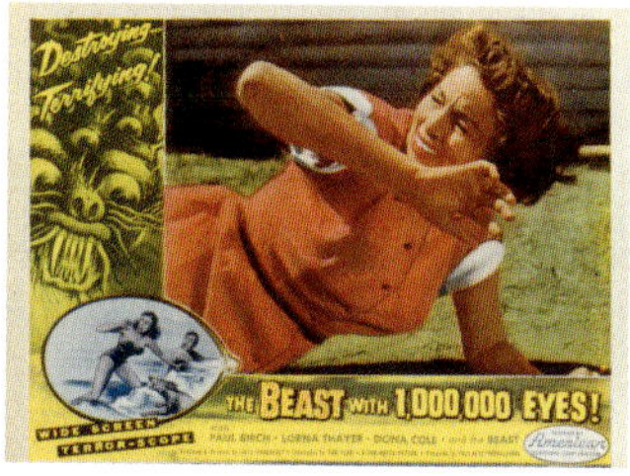 271

264-271. THE BEAST WITH 1,000,000 EYES, 1955
lobby cards

272 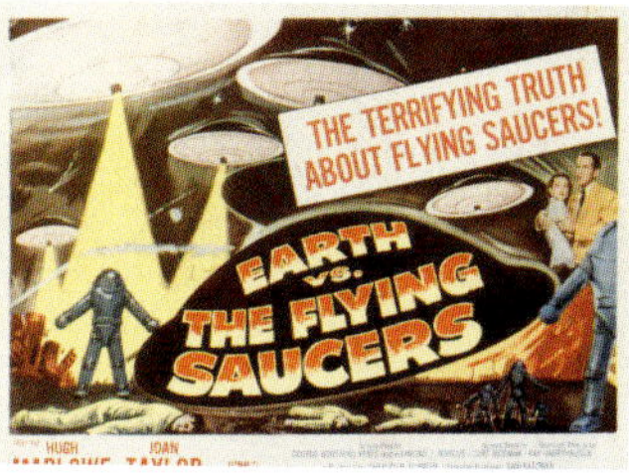

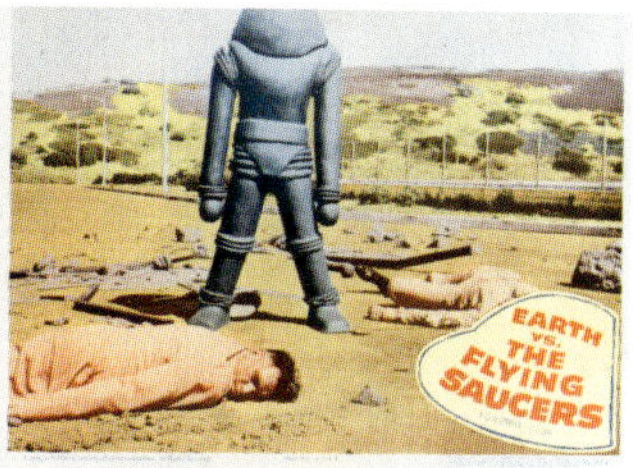 273

274 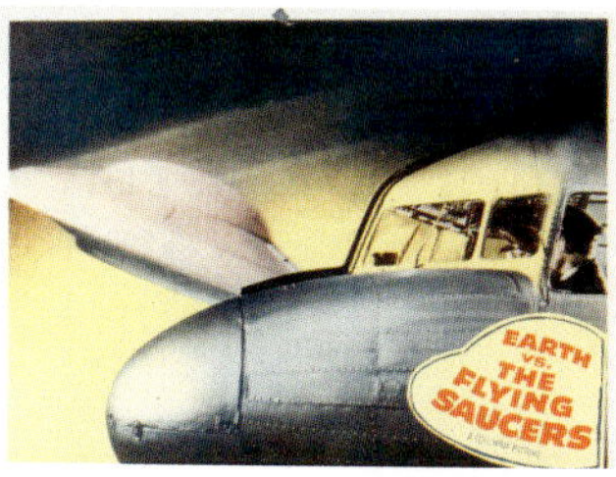

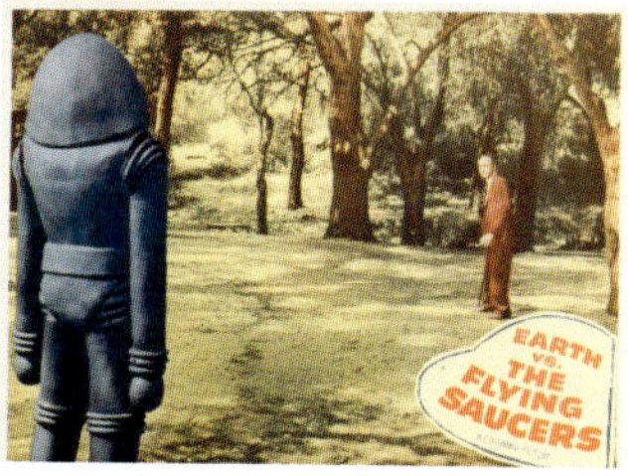 275

276 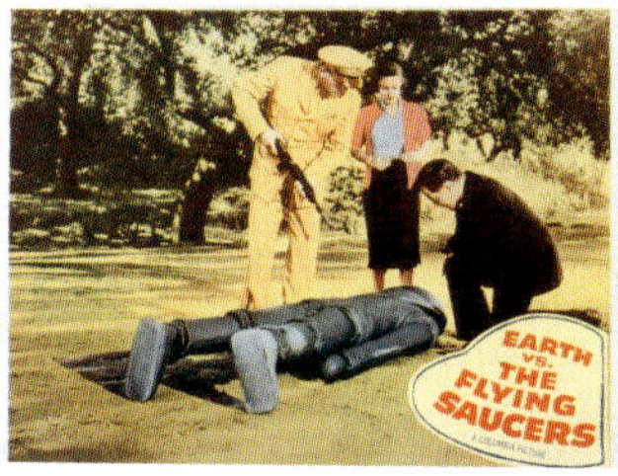

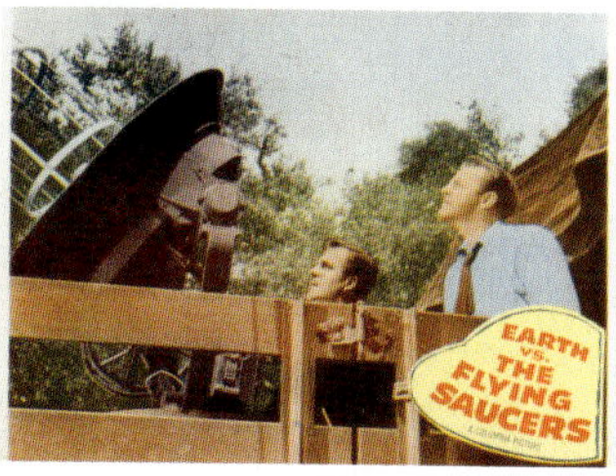 277

278 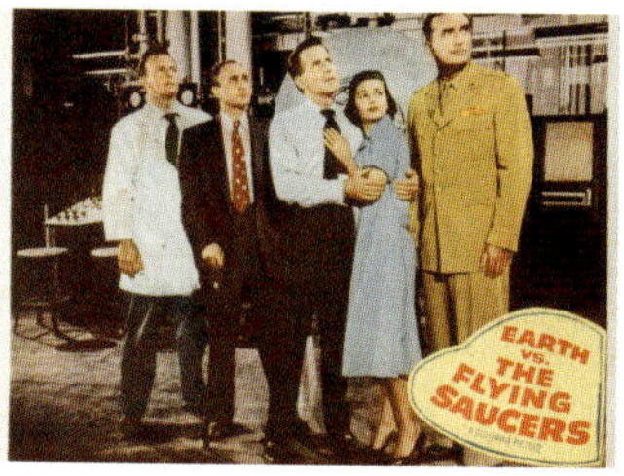

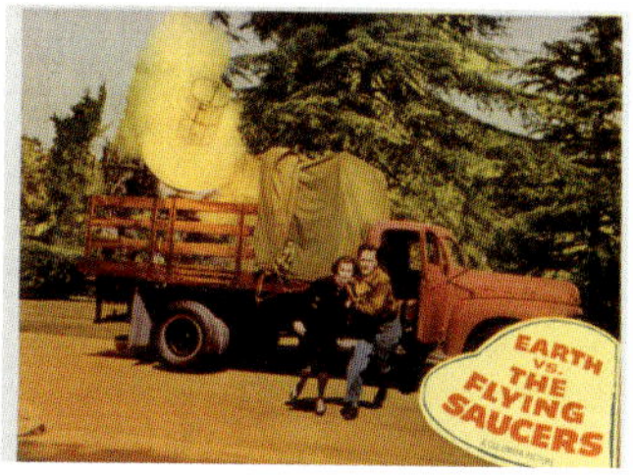 279

272-279. EARTH VS THE FLYING SAUCERS, 1956,
lobby cards

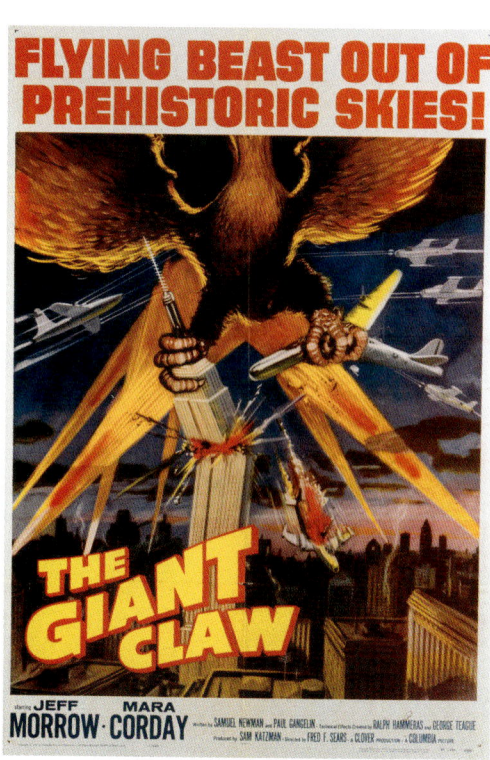

280. THE GIANT CLAW, 1957

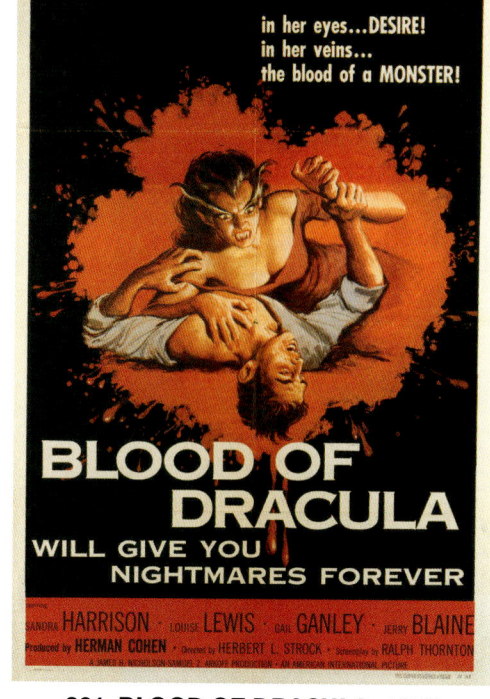

281. BLOOD OF DRACULA, 1957

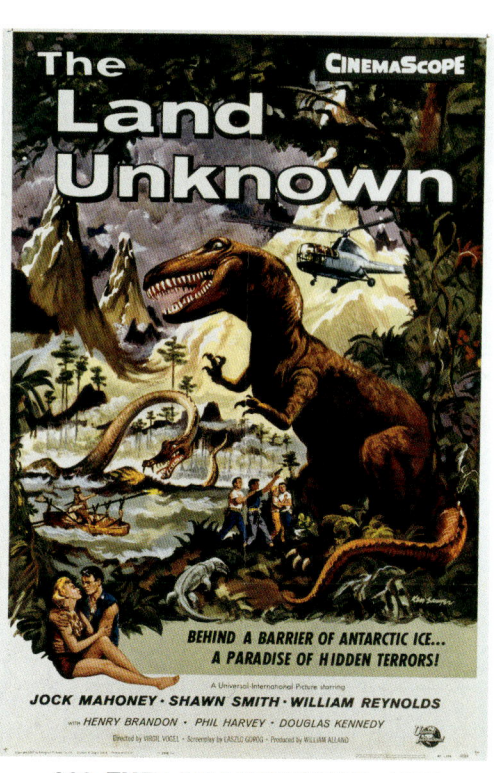

282. THE LAND UNKNOWN, 1957

283. FORBIDDEN PLANET, 1956

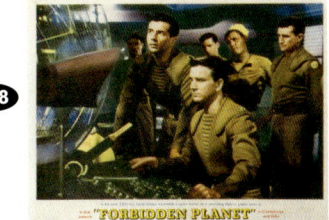

284-291. FORBIDDEN PLANET, 1956, lobby cards

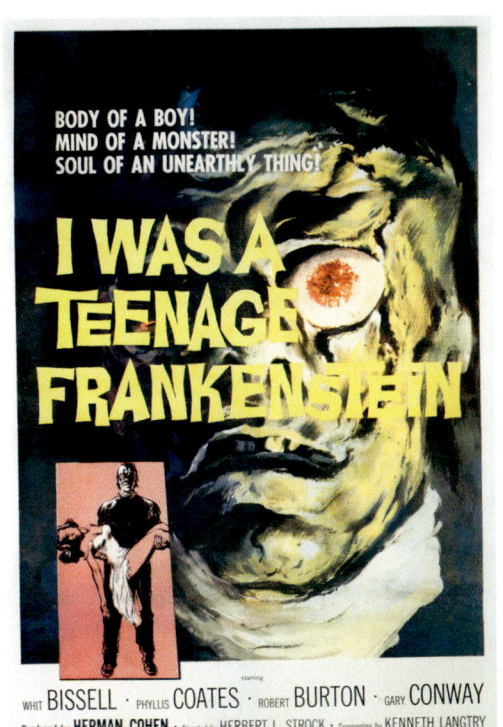

292. I WAS A TEENAGE FRANKENSTEIN, 1957

293. THE CRAWLING EYE, 1958

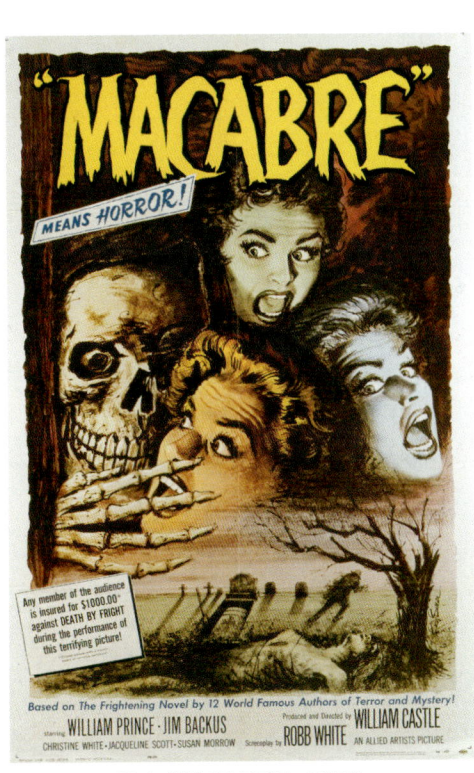
294. MACABRE, 1958

295. THIS ISLAND EARTH, 1955

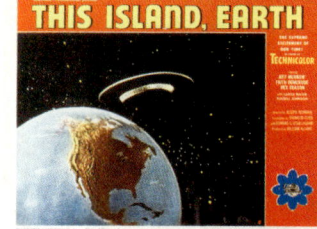 

296-303. THIS ISLAND EARTH, 1955, lobby cards

304. THE THING THAT COULDN'T DIE, 1958

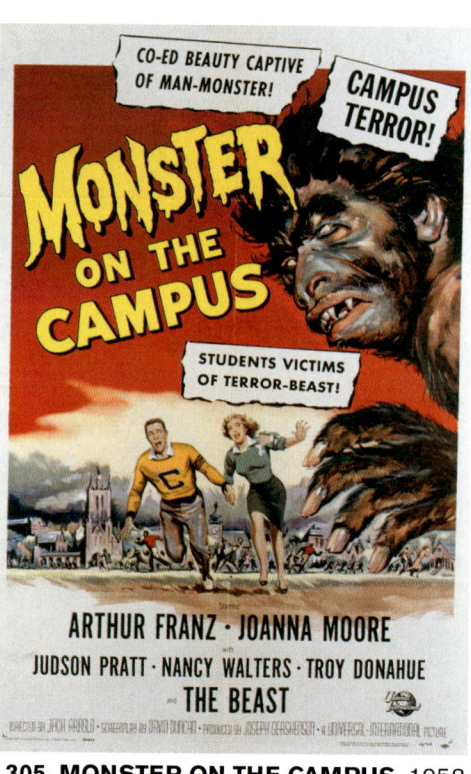

305. MONSTER ON THE CAMPUS, 1958

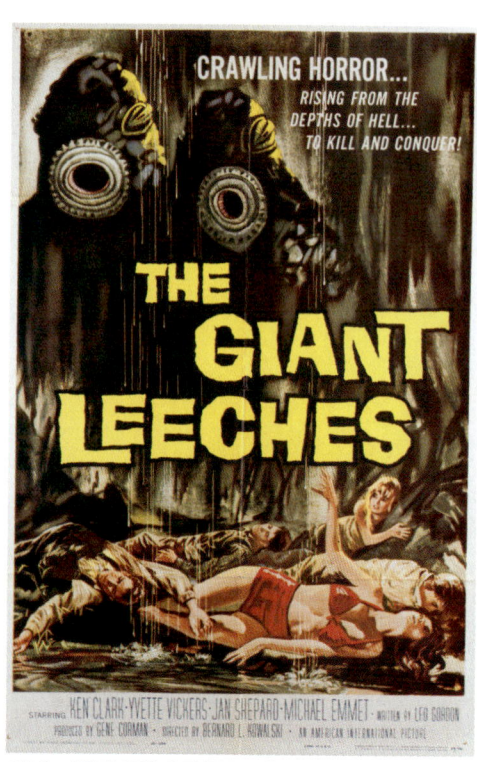

306. ATTACK OF THE GIANT LEECHES, 1959

307. TARANTULA, 1955

 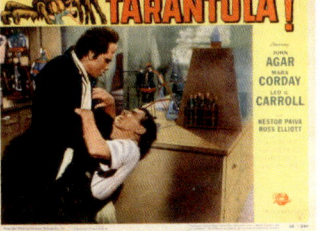
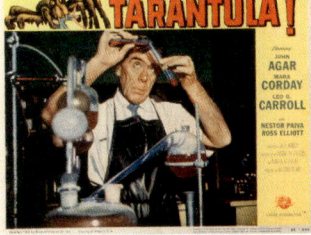 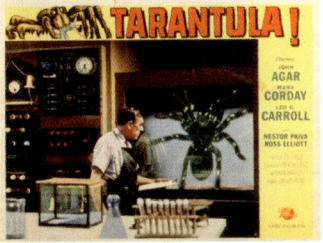
 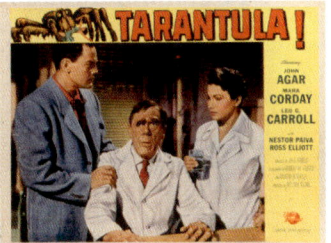

308-315. TARANTULA, 1955, lobby cards

316. TARANTULA, 1955, Forty By Sixty

317. IT CAME FROM OUTER SPACE, 1953

318. IT CAME FROM OUTER SPACE, 1953

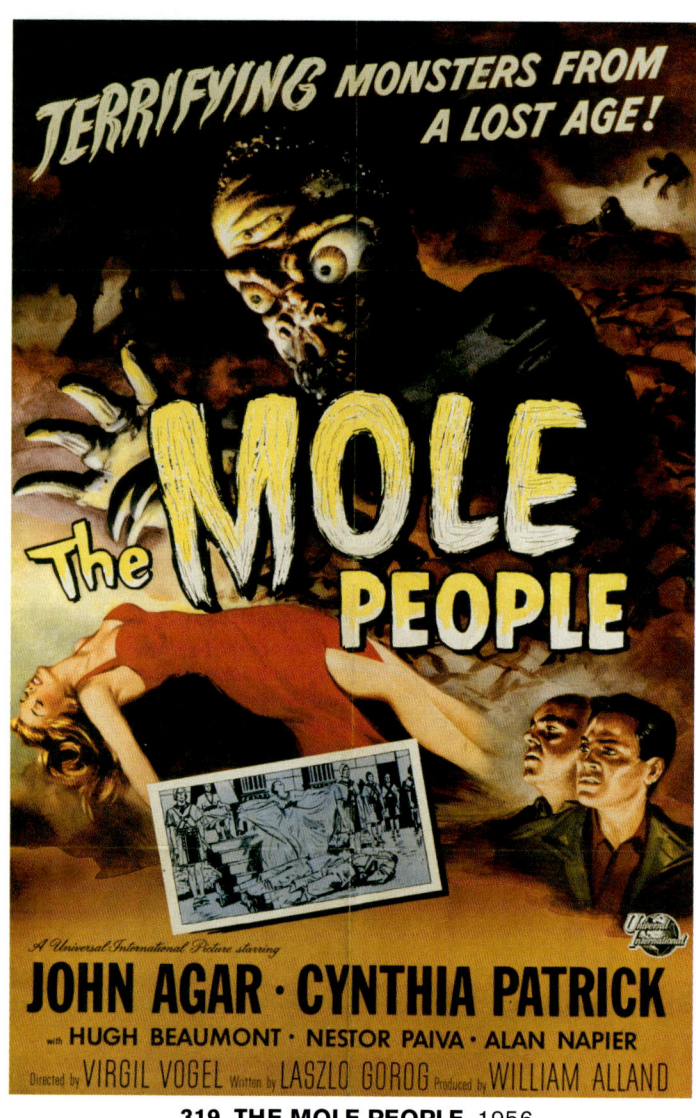

319. THE MOLE PEOPLE, 1956

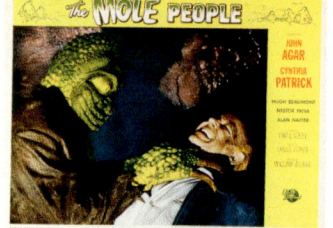
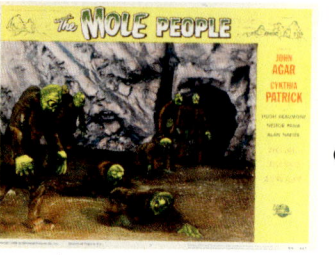

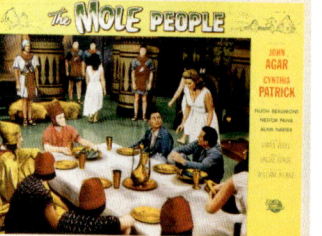

320-327. THE MOLE PEOPLE, 1956, lobby cards

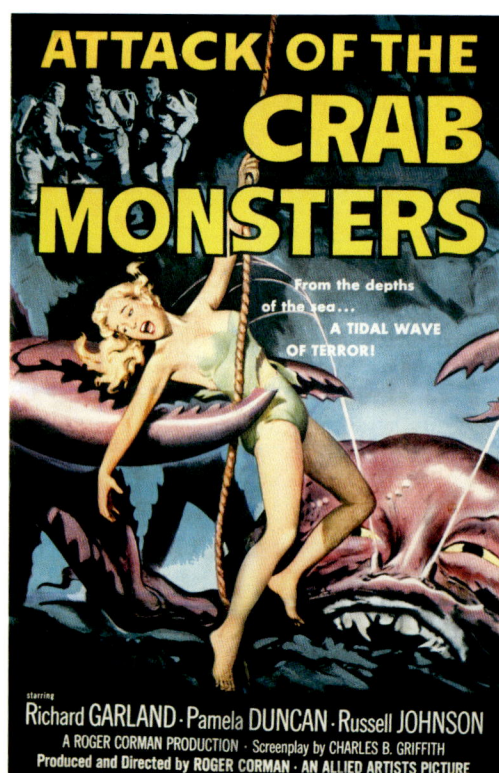

328. ATTACK OF THE CRAB MONSTERS, 1957

329-332. ATTACK OF THE CRAB MONSTERS, 1957, lobby cards

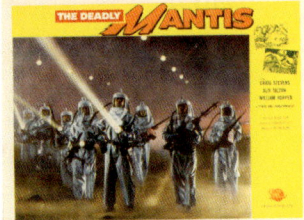
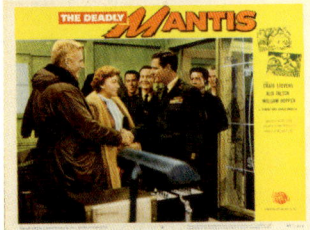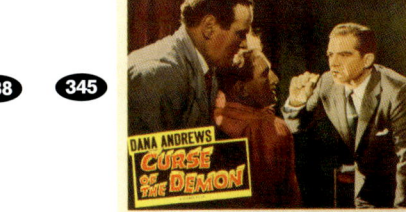

333-340. THE DEADLY MANTIS, 1957, lobby cards

341-348. NIGHT OF THE DEMON, 1957, lobby cards

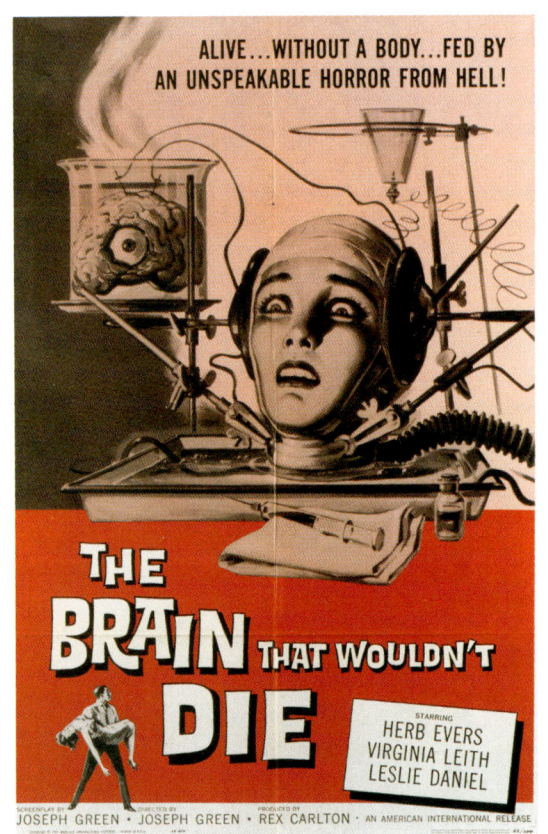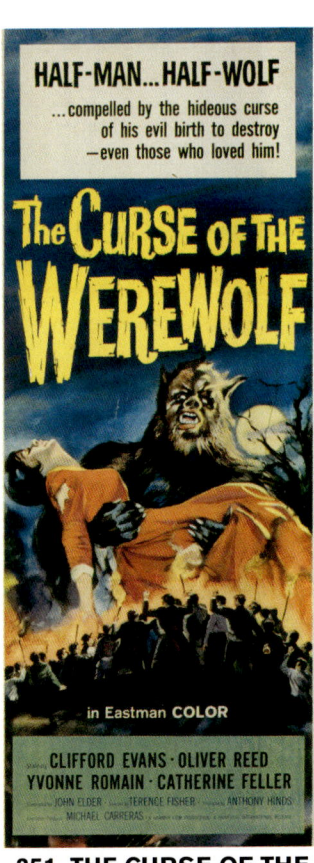

349. THE BRAIN THAT WOULDN'T DIE, 1962

350. THE RAVEN, 1963

351. THE CURSE OF THE WEREWOLF, 1961, insert

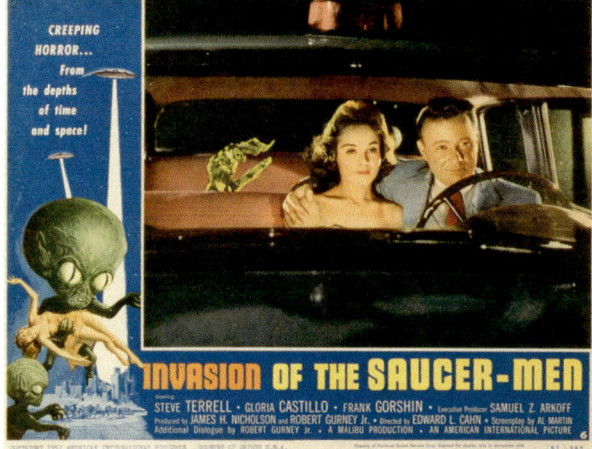

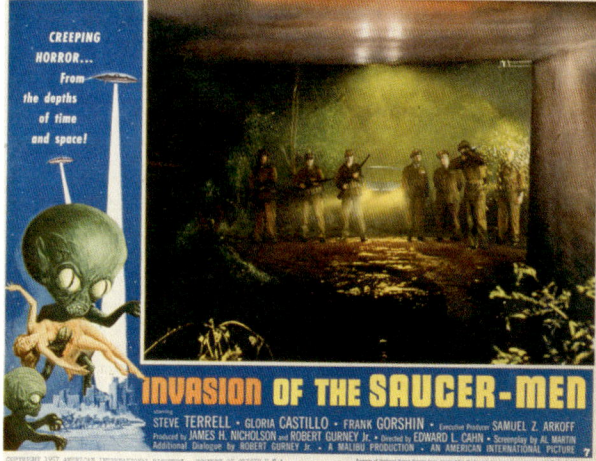

352-359. INVASION OF THE SAUCER-MEN, 1957, lobby cards

360. PLAN 9 FROM OUTER SPACE, 1958

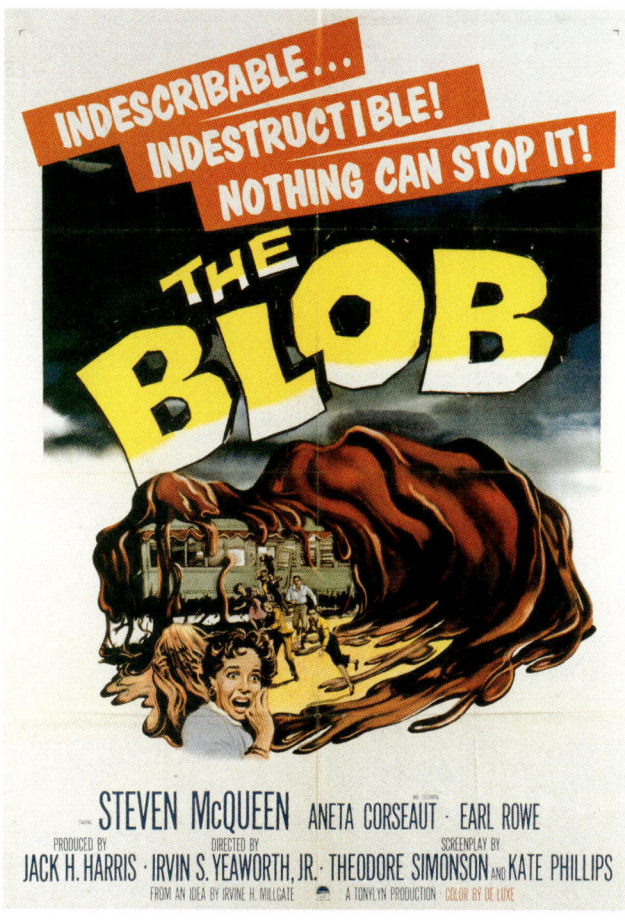

361. THE BLOB, 1956

362

363

364

365

366

367

368

369

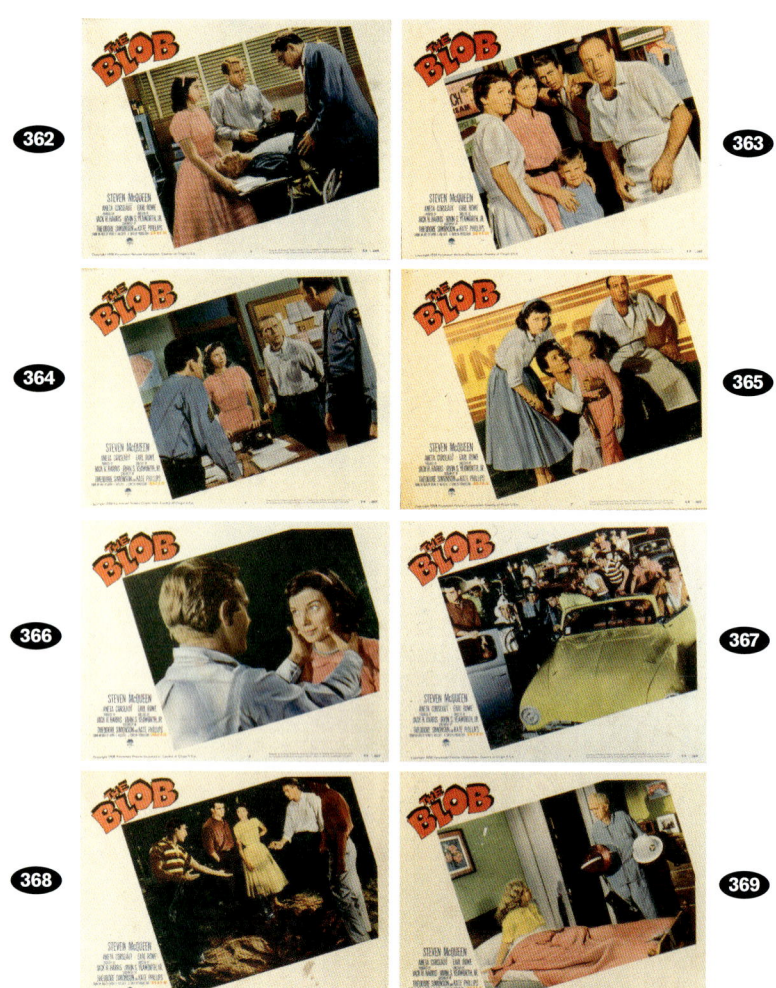

362-369. THE BLOB, 1958, lobby cards

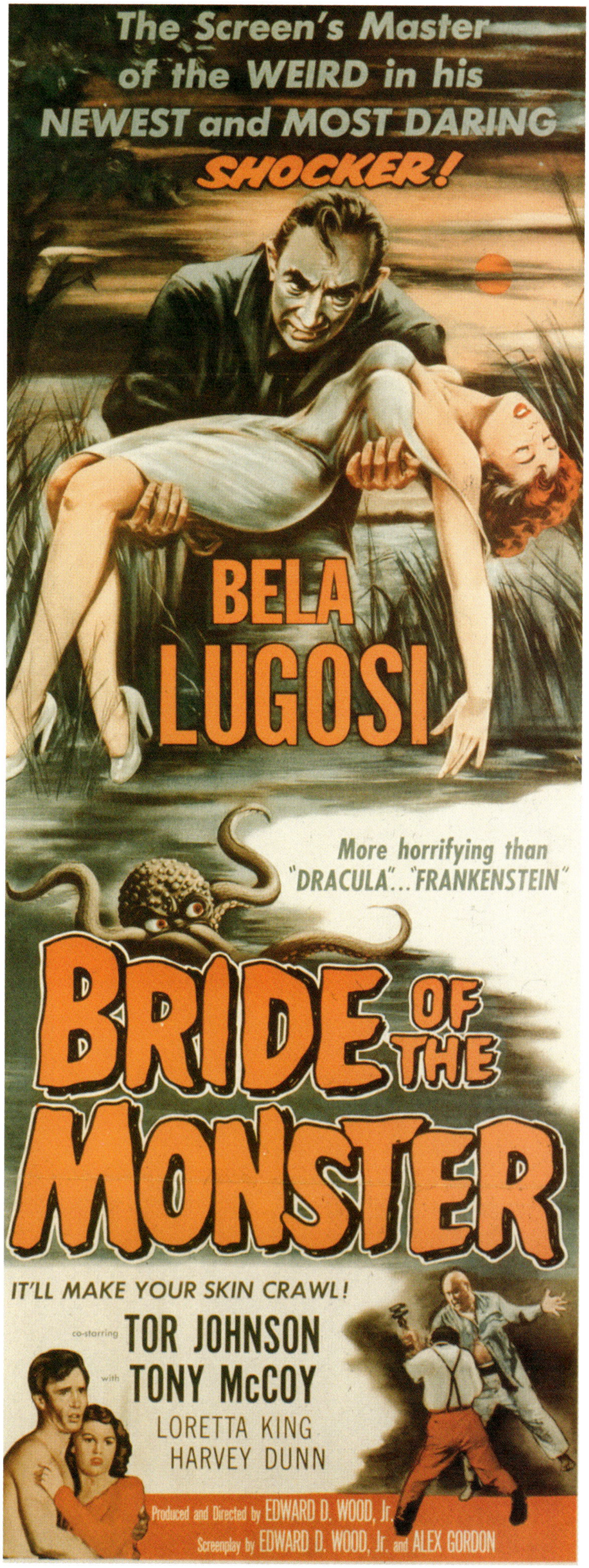

370. BRIDE OF THE MONSTER, 1956, insert

371. CREATURE FROM THE BLACK LAGOON, 1954, half-sheet

372. CREATURE FROM THE BLACK LAGOON, 1954, title lobby card

373. INVASION OF THE SAUCER-MEN, 1957, half-sheet

374. BEAST FROM HAUNTED CAVE/THE WASP WOMAN, British quad, double-bill release

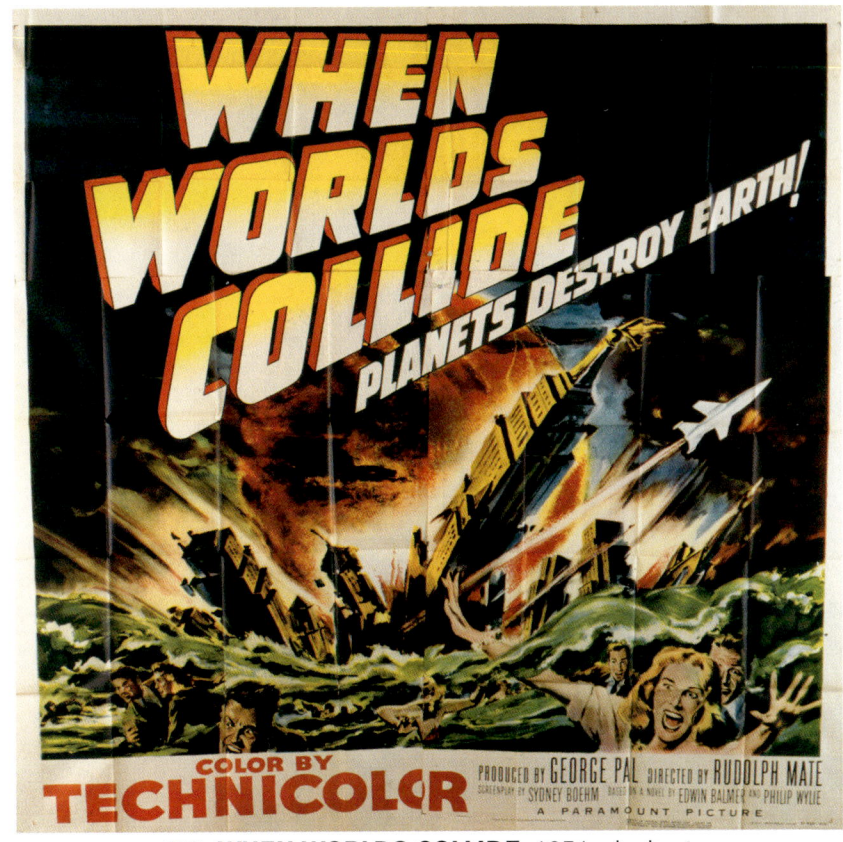

375. WHEN WORLDS COLLIDE, 1951, six-sheet

376
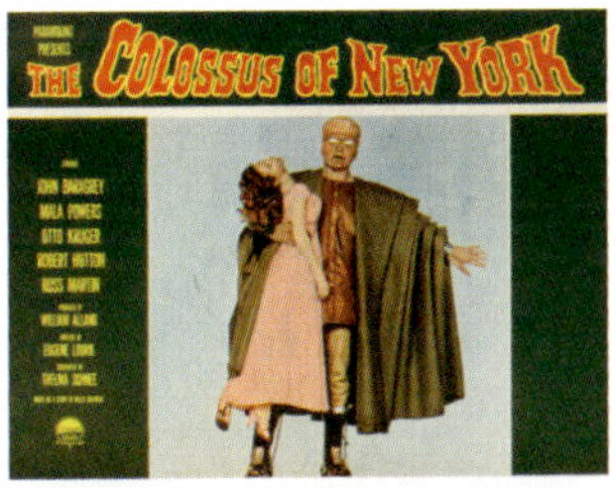

377
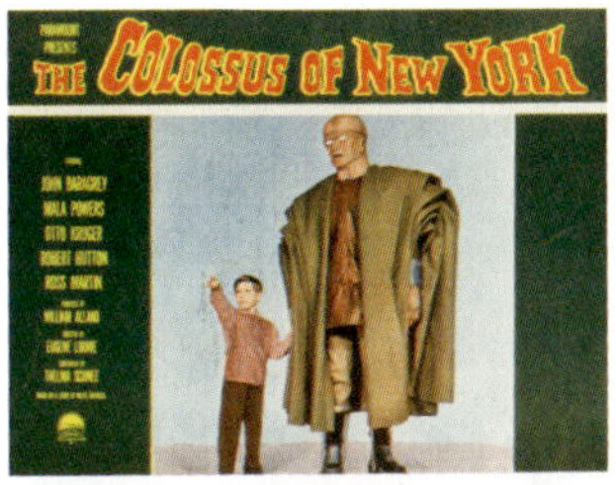

378
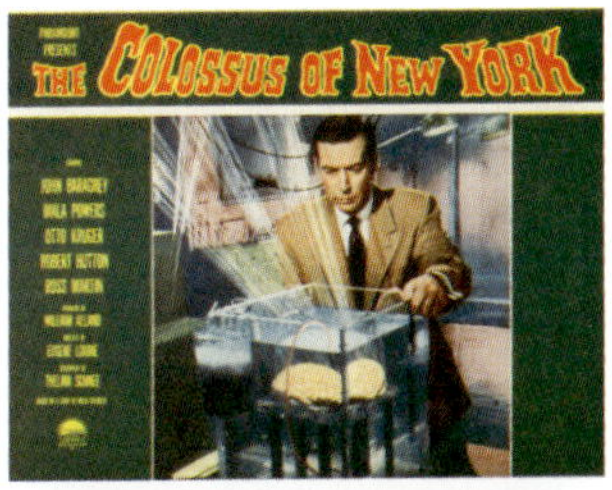

379
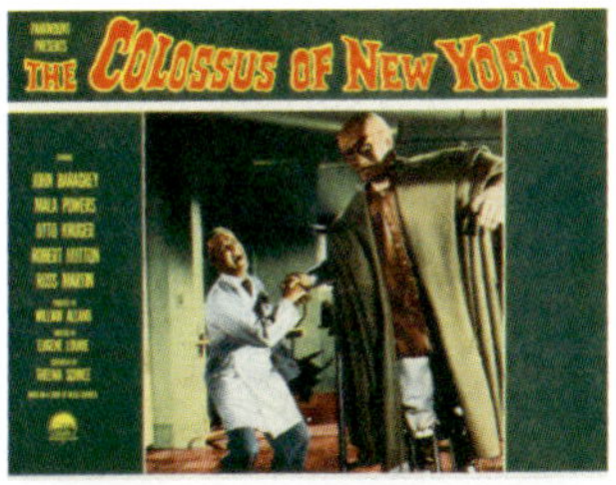

380
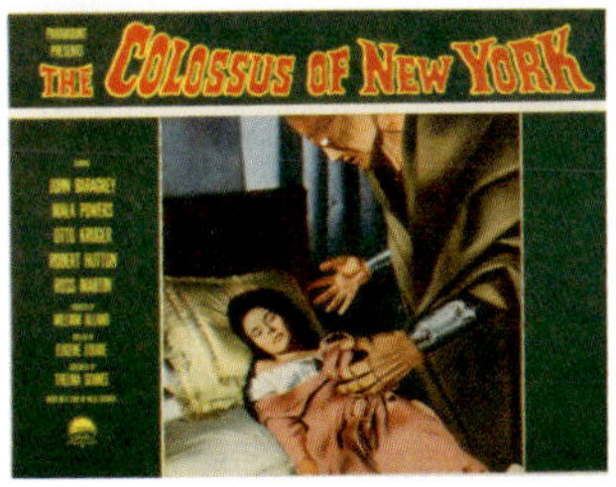

381
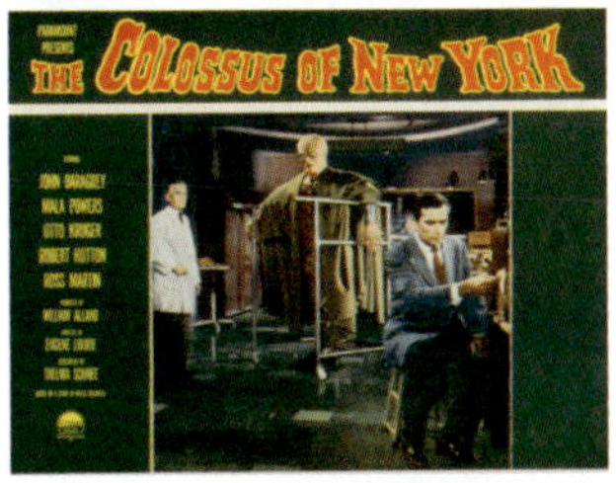

382
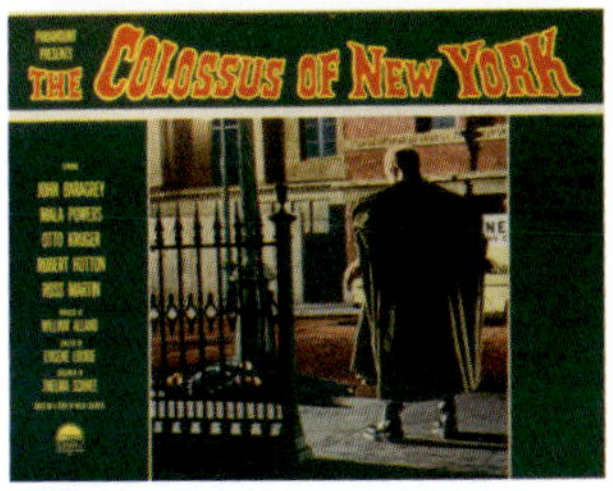

383
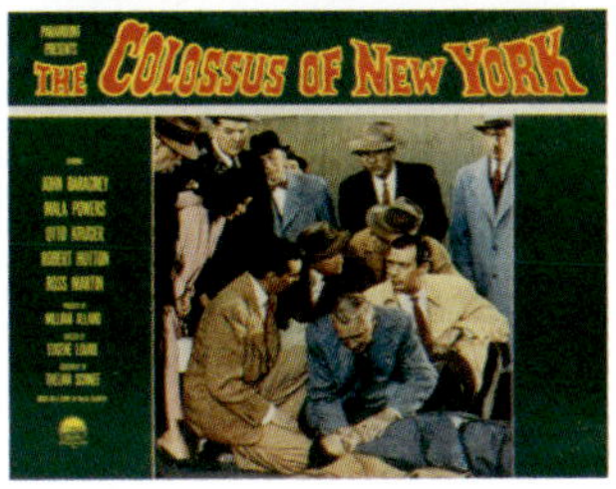

376-383. THE COLOSSUS OF NEW YORK, 1958, lobby cards

384
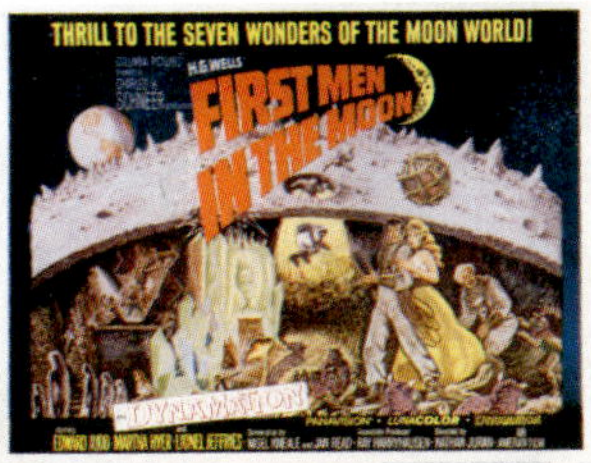

385
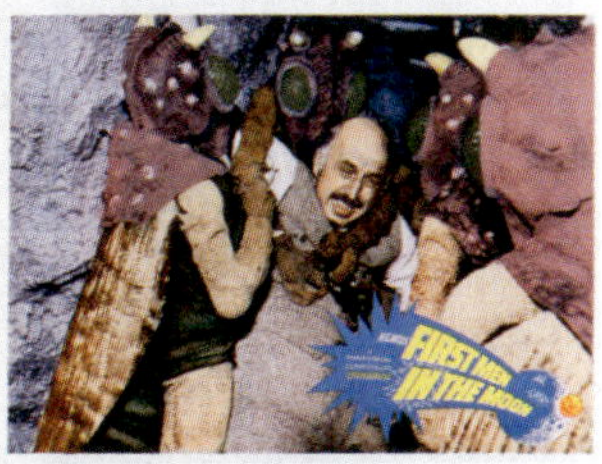

386
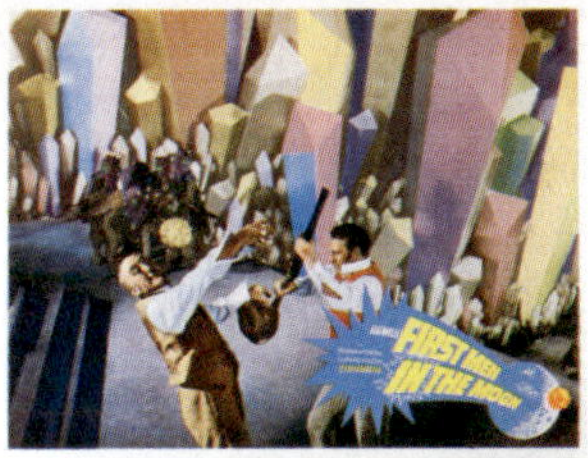

387
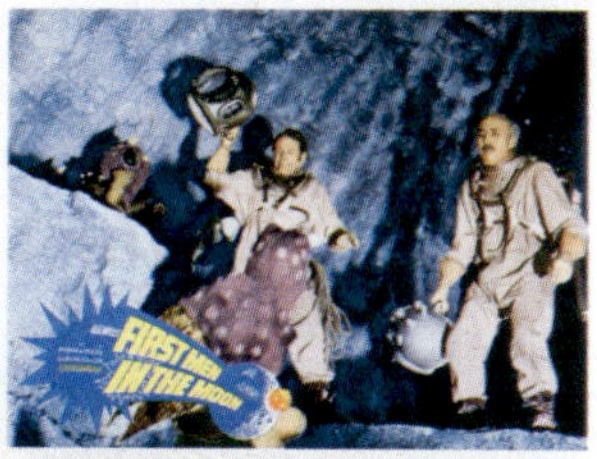

388
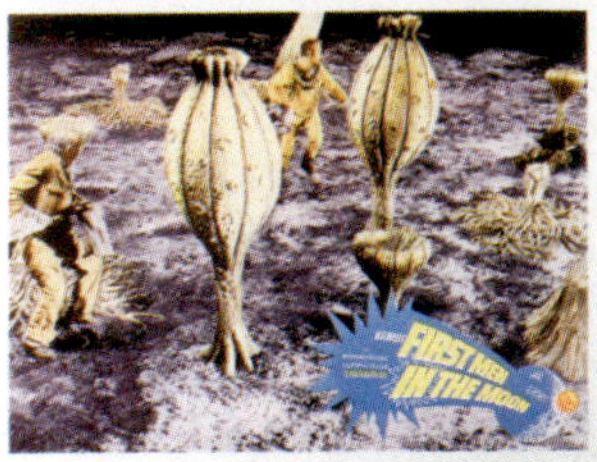

389
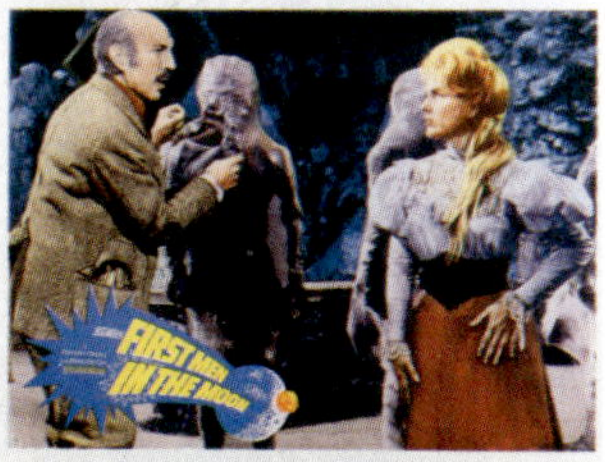

390
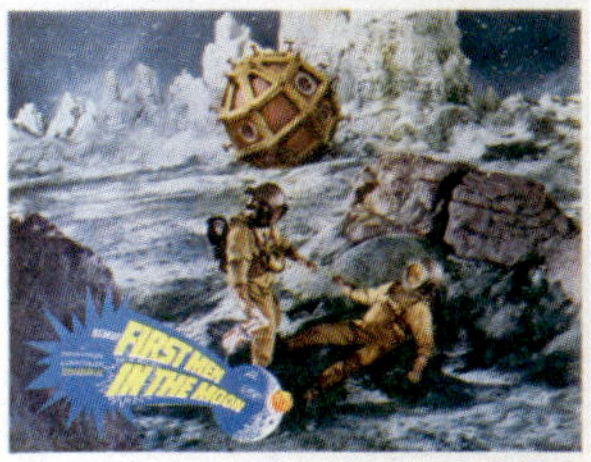

391
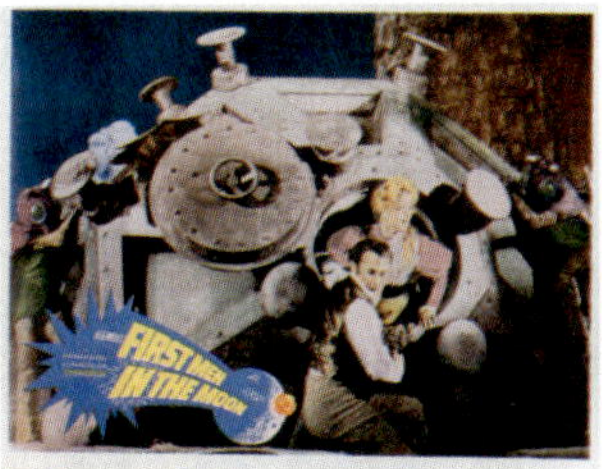

384-391. FIRST MEN IN THE MOON, 1964, lobby cards

392. THE SHE-CREATURE, 1956, half-sheet

393. THE BLACK SLEEP, 1956, half-sheet

394. THE LAND UNKNOWN, 1957, half-sheet

395. I MARRIED A MONSTER FROM OUTER SPACE, 1958, half-sheet

396. THE ASTOUNDING SHE MONSTER, 1958, half-sheet

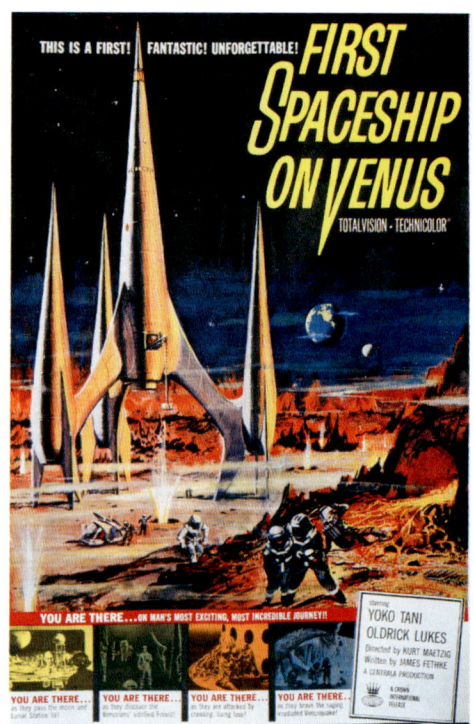
397. FIRST SPACESHIP ON VENUS, 1962

398. ATTACK OF THE 50 FT. WOMAN, 1958, insert

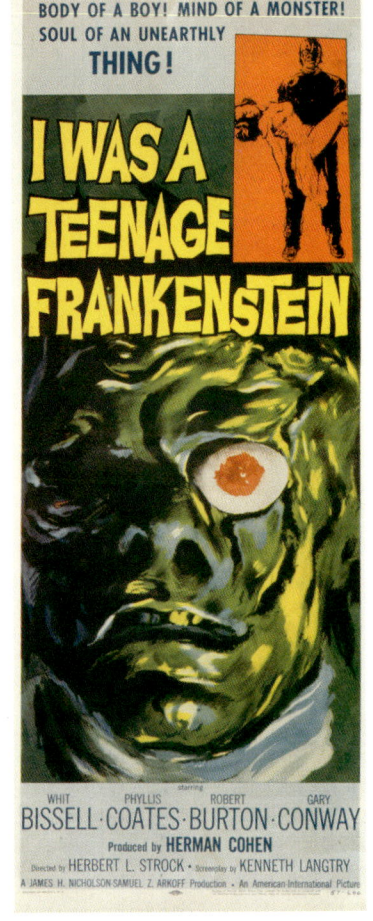

399. I WAS A TEENAGE WEREWOLF, 1957, insert

400. I WAS A TEENAGE FRANKENSTEIN, 1957, insert

401. FROM HELL IT CAME, 1957, insert

402. THE GIANT BEHEMOTH, 1959, insert

403. THE MOLE PEOPLE, 1956, insert

404. ATTACK OF THE CRAB MONSTERS, 1957, insert

405. THE CREATURE WALKS AMONG US, 1956, insert

406. IT CONQUERED THE WORLD, 1956, insert

407. THE SHE-CREATURE, 1956, insert

408. PSYCHO, 1960, six-sheet

409. PSYCHO, 1960, insert

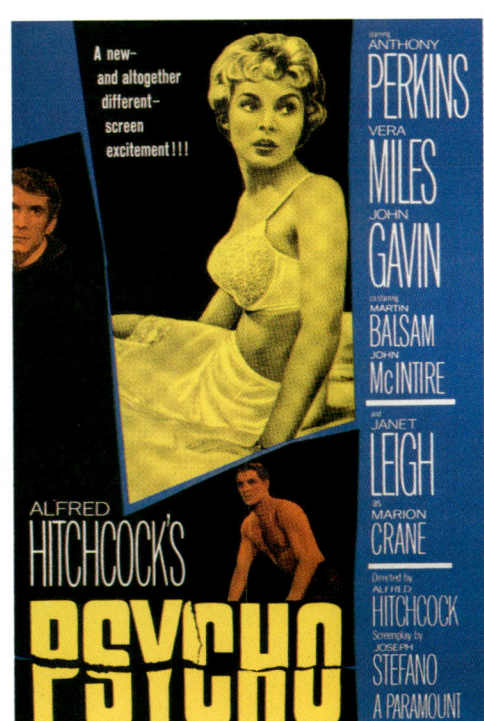

410. PSYCHO, 1960

411. THE CURSE OF THE WEREWOLF, 1961

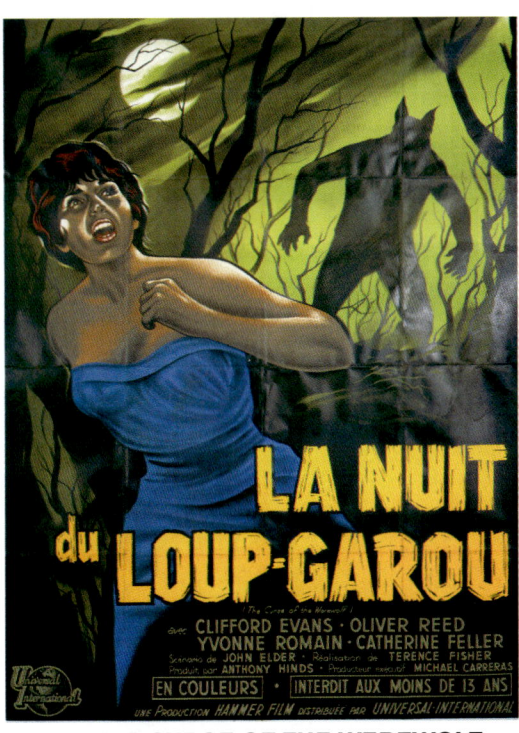

412. THE CURSE OF THE WEREWOLF, 1961, French, one-panel

413. A HARD DAY'S NIGHT, 1964, British quad

414. LA NOTTE, 1961, Italian 13.25x37.75

415. THE BICYCLE THIEF, 1948, 1955 reissue Italian, two-panel

416. BOB LE FLAMBEUR, 1955, French

417. LA DOLCE VITA, 1961, Italian one-sheet

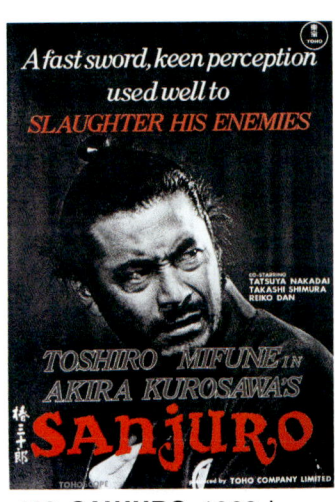
418. SANJURO, 1962 Japan

419. IL BOOM, 1963, Italian, two-panel

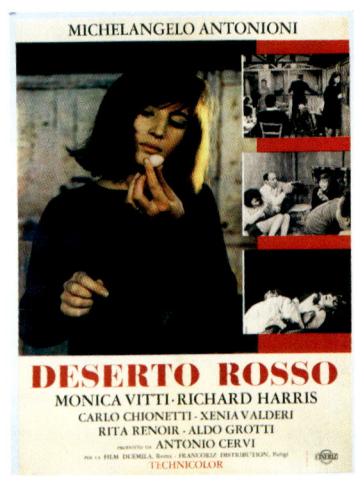
420. RED DESERT, 1964, Italian large photobusta

421. UMBRELLAS OF CHERBOURG, 1965, French

422. THE BRIDE WORE BLACK 1968, French

423. BREAKER MORANT, 1980, Australian one-sheet

424. FANNY AND ALEXANDER, 1982, Swedish

425. COME AND SEE, 1985, German

426. GUN CRAZY, 1950, three-sheet

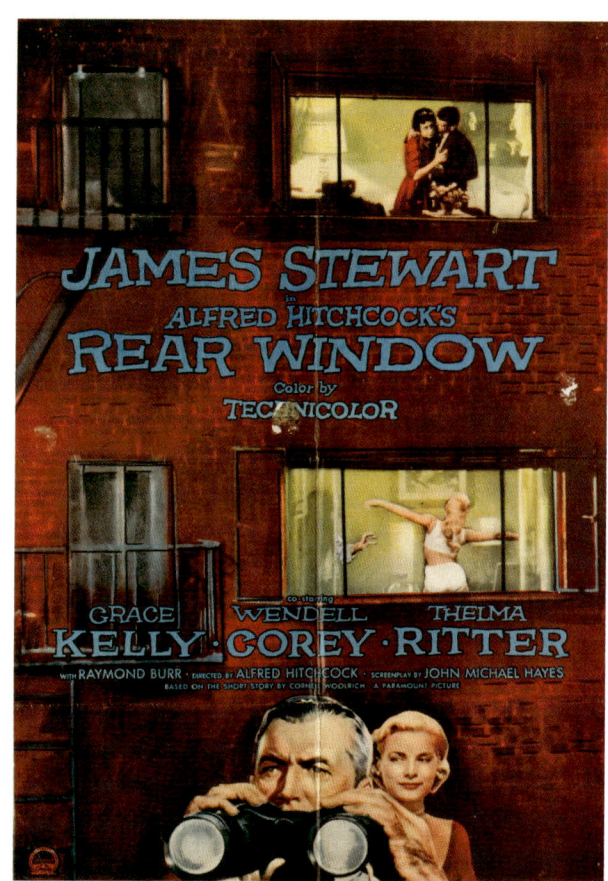

427. REAR WINDOW, 1954

428. THE PRINCE AND THE SHOWGIRL, 1957

429. A PLACE IN THE SUN, 1951, paper banner

430. DON'T BOTHER TO KNOCK, 1952, paper banner

431. SUNSET BLVD, 1950, German 33x47

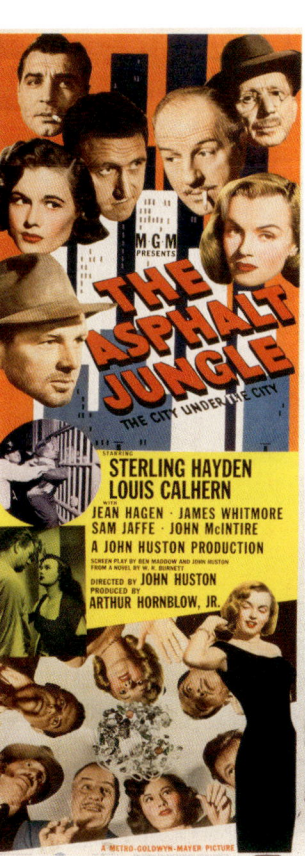

432. THE ASPHALT JUNGLE, 1950, insert

433. NIAGARA, 1953

434. REBEL WITHOUT A CAUSE, 1955

435. SINGIN' IN THE RAIN, 1952, lobby card, autographed by Gene Kelly

436. AN AMERICAN IN PARIS, 1951

437. THE WILD ONE, 1953

438. HIGH NOON, 1952, Argentinean

439. DAVY CROCKETT, KING OF THE WILD FRONTIER, 1955

440. JAILHOUSE ROCK, 1957, Argentinean

441. REBEL WITHOUT A CAUSE, 1955, insert

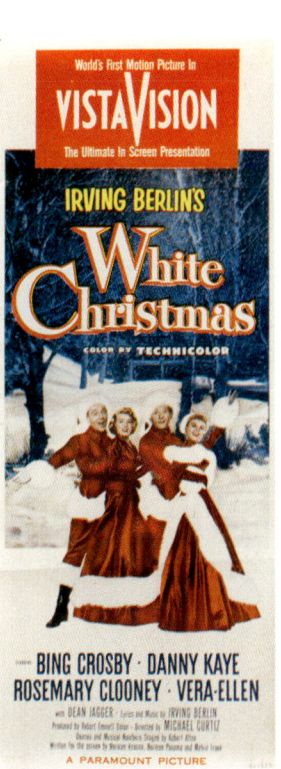

442. WHITE CHRISTMAS, 1954, insert

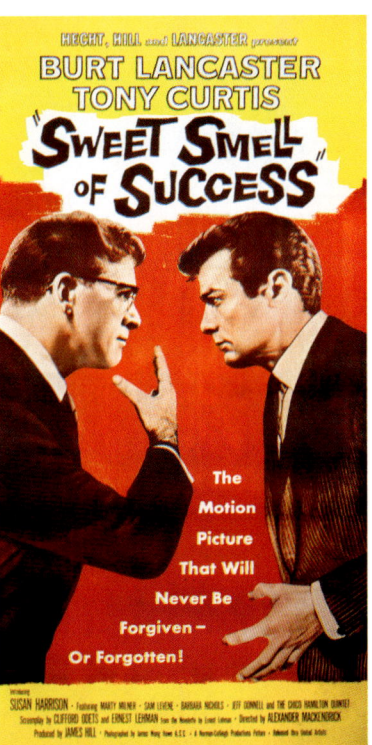

443. SWEET SMELL OF SUCCESS, 1957, three-sheet

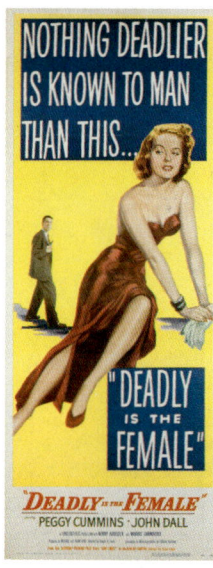
444. DEADLY IS THE FEMALE, 1950, insert

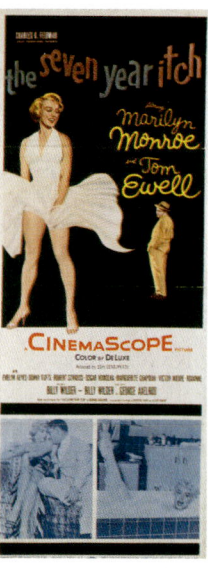
445. THE SEVEN YEAR ITCH, 1955, insert

446. HOT ROD GIRL, 1956, insert

447. LIANE, JUNGLE GODDESS, 1958, insert

448. COOL AND THE CRAZY, 1958

449. MAN BAIT, 1952 half-sheet

450. UNDERWATER, 1955

451. GLEN OR GLENDA, 1953

452. SOULS IN PAWN, 1940

453. FRIGID WIFE, 1950, two-sheet

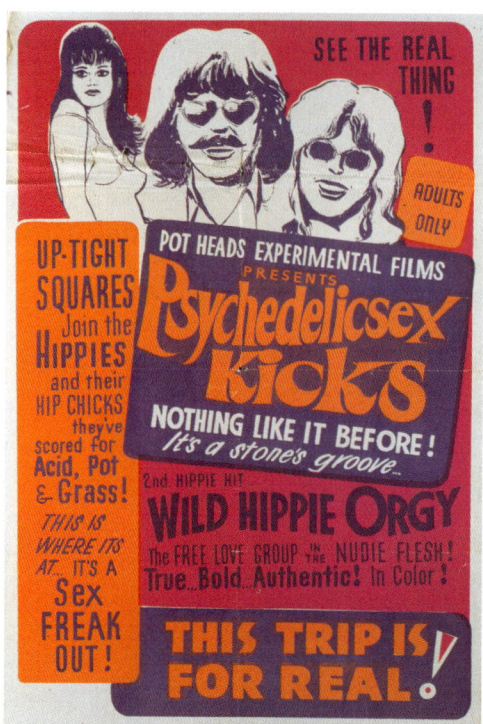
454. PSYCHEDELIC SEX KICKS, 1960

455. PAYMENT ON DEMAND, 1951, half-sheet

456. ROCK 'N' ROLL REVUE, 1955, half-sheet

457. REAR WINDOW, 1954, Italian, locandina

458. TO CATCH A THIEF, 1955, Italian, locandina

459. THE KILLING, 1956, half-sheet

460. THE SEVENTH VOYAGE OF SINBAD, 1958, Russian

461. NORTH BY NORTHWEST, 1959, Belgian

462. BEN-HUR, 1960, poster

463. PERSONA, 1967, British quad

464. FAHRENHEIT 451, 1967, British quad

465. BLACK ORPHEUS, 1960, Polish

466. THE TIME MACHINE, 1960

467. SPARTACUS, 1961 Polish

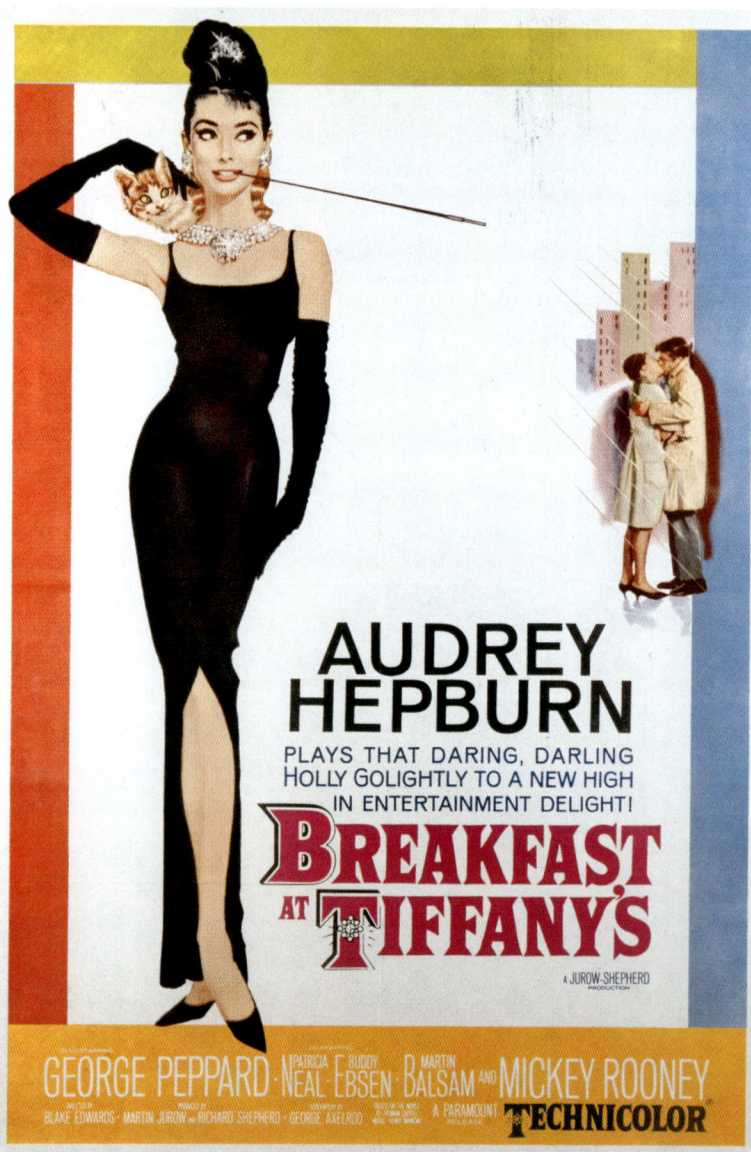
468. BREAKFAST AT TIFFANY'S, 1961

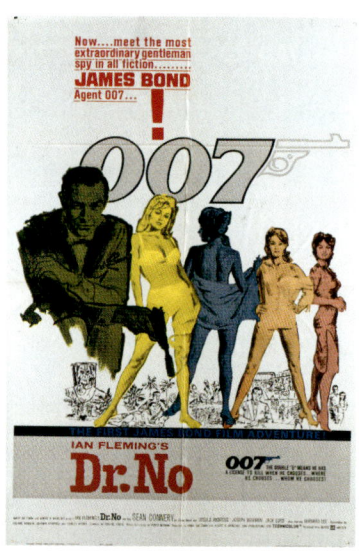
469. DR NO, 1962

470. ONE, TWO, THREE, 1962, three-sheet

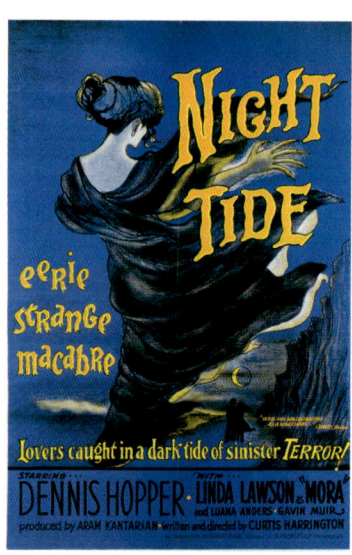
471. NIGHT TIDE, 1963

472. BLOOD FEAST, 1963

473. TO KILL A MOCKINGBIRD, 1963

474. TO KILL A MOCKINGBIRD, 1963

475. TO KILL A MOCKINGBIRD, 1963, Romanian

476. MARY POPPINS, 1964, two door-panels

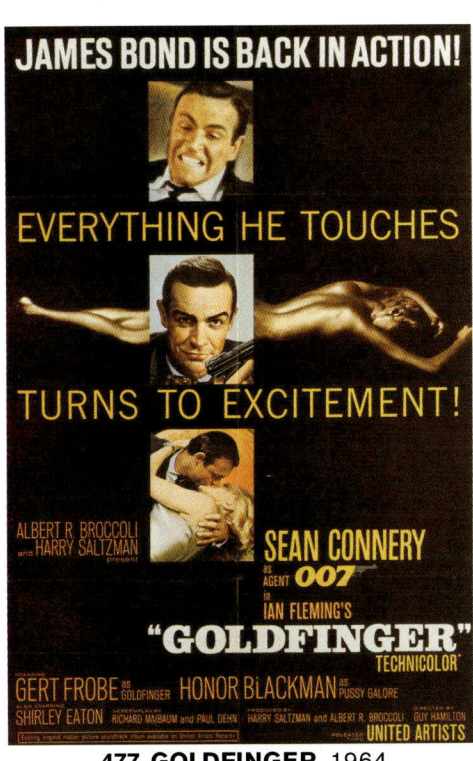
477. GOLDFINGER, 1964

478. FROM RUSSIA WITH LOVE, 1964, Japanese

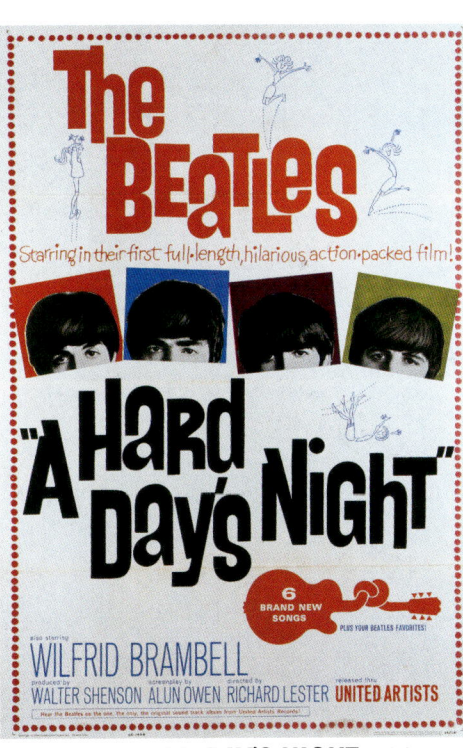
479. A HARD DAY'S NIGHT, 1964

480. ALPHAVILLE, 1965, Japanese

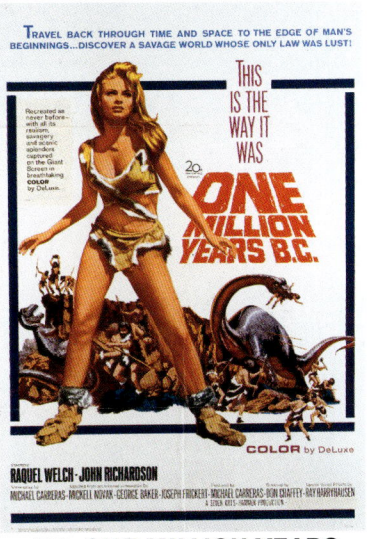
481. ONE MILLION YEARS BC, 1966

482. SECONDS, 1966 insert

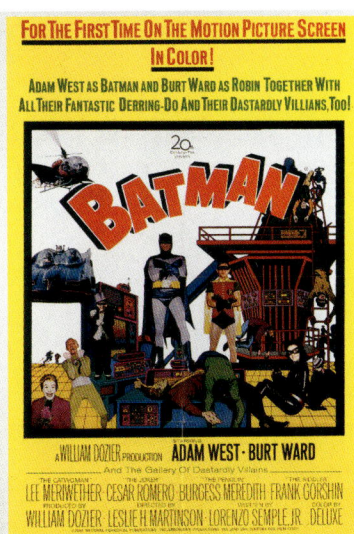
483. BATMAN, 1966

484. SHE FREAK, 1967

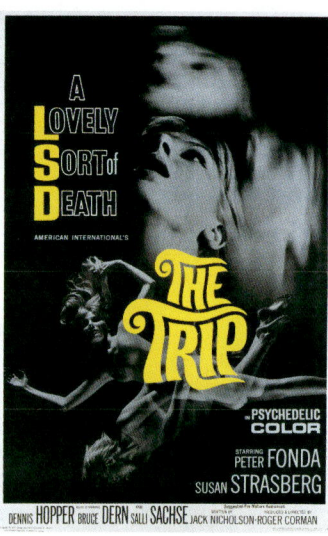
485. THE TRIP, 1967

486. FANTASTIC VOYAGE, 1966, special poster

487. A MAN AND A WOMAN, 1966, Japanese

488. A FISTFUL OF DOLLARS, 1967

489. A FISTFUL OF DOLLARS, 1967

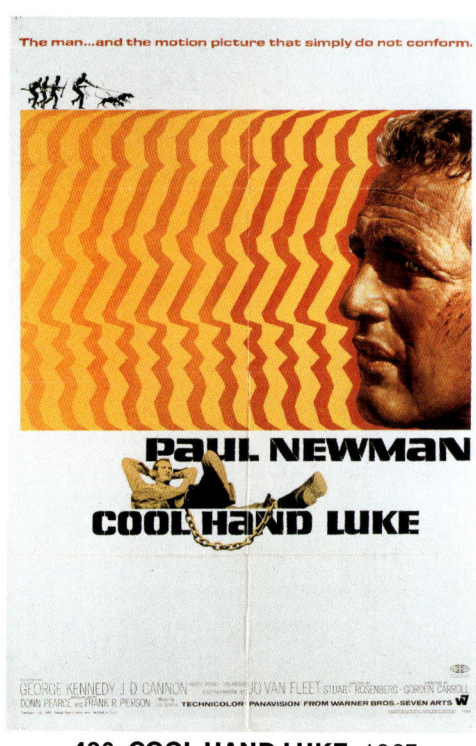
490. COOL HAND LUKE, 1967

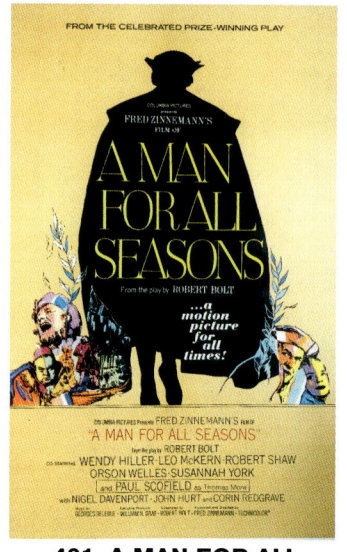
491. A MAN FOR ALL SEASONS, 1967

492. THE PRODUCERS, 1967

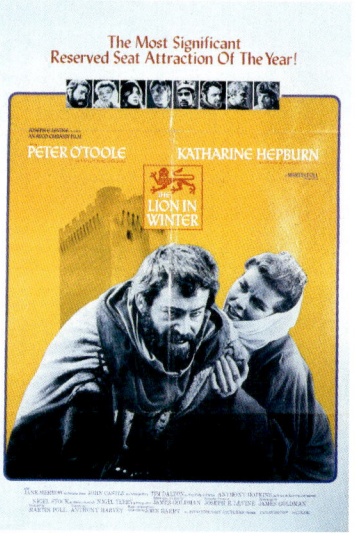
493. THE LION IN WINTER, 1968

494. PLANET OF THE APES, 1968

495. BULLITT, 1969

496. BULLITT, 1969

497. BULLITT, 1969, East German

498. DOWNHILL RACER 1969

499. DOWNHILL RACER, 1969

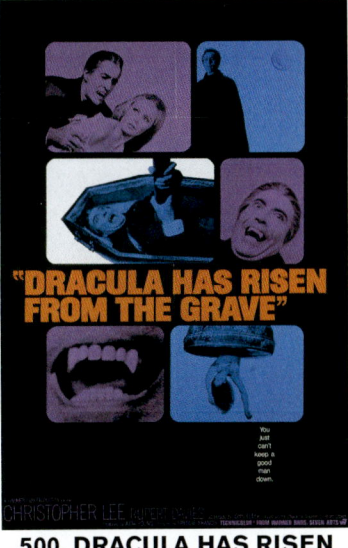
500. DRACULA HAS RISEN FROM THE GRAVE, 1969

501. MIDNIGHT COWBOY, 1969

502. PIERROT LE FOU, 1969, Japanese

503. SALESMAN, 1969

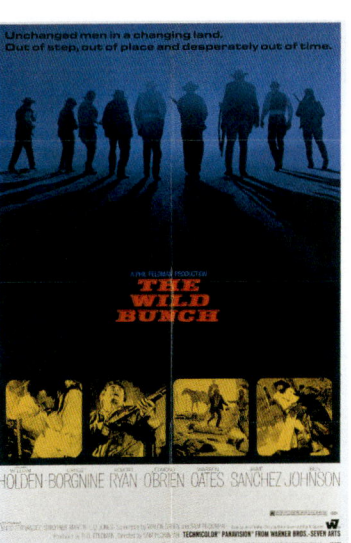
504. THE WILD BUNCH, 1969

505. DODESUKADEN, 1970, Japanese

506. KELLY'S HEROES, 1970

507. ON HER MAJESTY'S SECRET SERVICE, 1970, Japanese

508. a.k.a. CASSIUS CLAY, 1970

509. HELLO DOLLY, 1970

510. GET CARTER, 1971, Spanish one-sheet

511. DIRTY HARRY, 1971, Forty By Sixty

512. DIRTY HARRY, 1971

513. SHAFT, 1971, three-sheet

514. MAD DOGS AND ENGLISHMEN, 1971

515. WILLY WONKA AND THE CHOCOLATE FACTORY, 1971

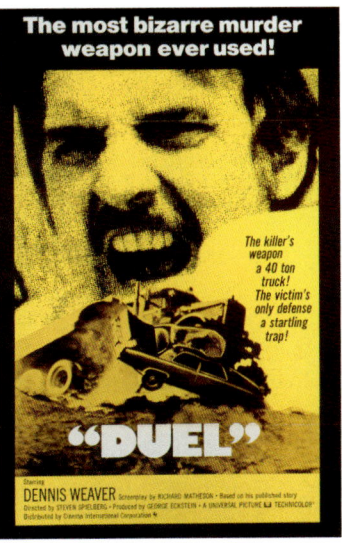
516. DUEL, 1972

517. CABARET, 1972, Russian

518. THE GETAWAY, 1972

519. THE GODSON, 1972, Japanese

520. ROBIN HOOD, 1973, set of 4 door panels

521. ENTER THE DRAGON, 1973

522. ENTER THE DRAGON, 1973, Japanese

523. THE LONG GOODBYE, 1973

524. THE LONG GOODBYE, 1973, insert

525. MAGNUM FORCE, 1973

526. MAGNUM FORCE, 1973, 20x28 poster

527. MAGNUM FORCE, 1973, Italian, one-sheet

528. WESTWORLD, 1973

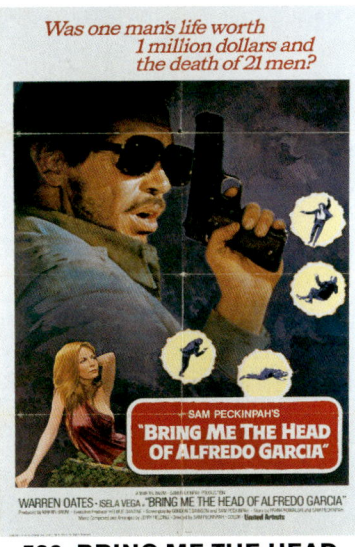
529. BRING ME THE HEAD OF ALFREDO GARCIA, 1974

530. DEATH WISH, 1974

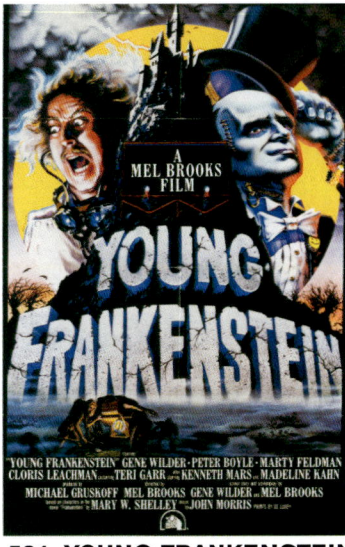
531. YOUNG FRANKENSTEIN, 1974

532. THE EXORCIST, 1974

533. DOG DAY AFTERNOON, 1975

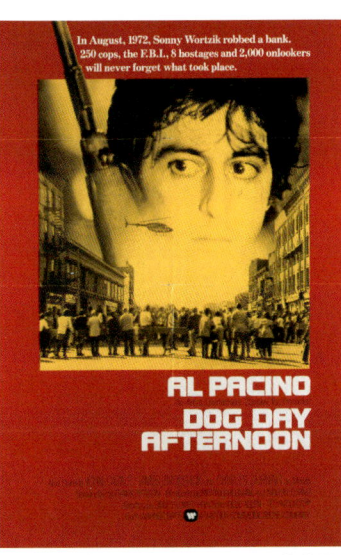
534. DOG DAY AFTERNOON, 1975

535. PUMPING IRON, 1977

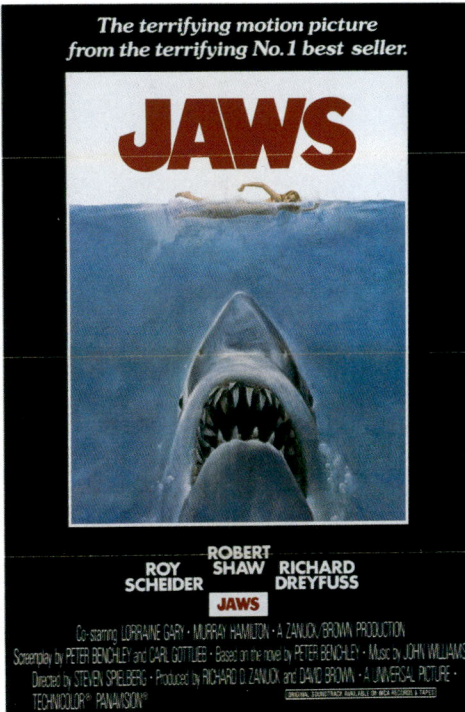
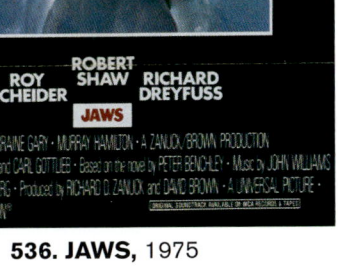
536. JAWS, 1975

537. THE OUTLAW JOSEY WALES, 1976, special advance poster

538. THE OUTLAW JOSEY WALES, 1976

539. THE SPY WHO LOVED ME, 1977, Japanese

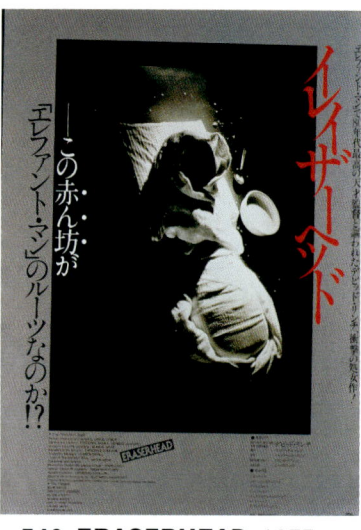
540. ERASERHEAD, 1977, Japanese

541. GREASE, 1978

542. GREASE, 1978

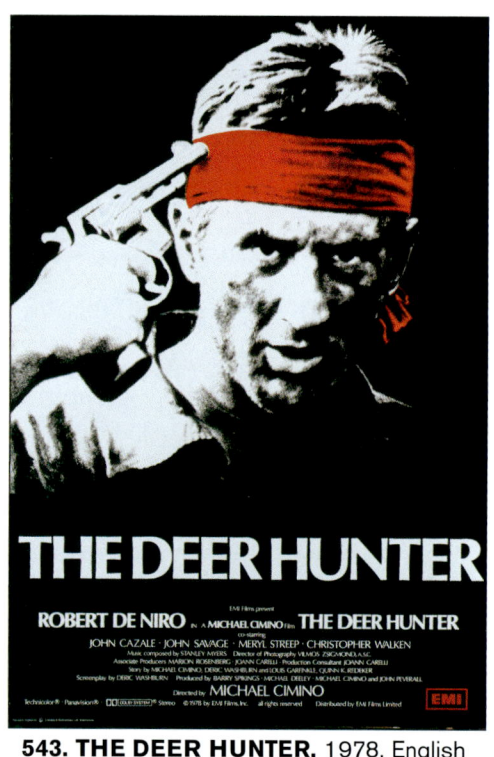
543. THE DEER HUNTER, 1978, English one-sheet

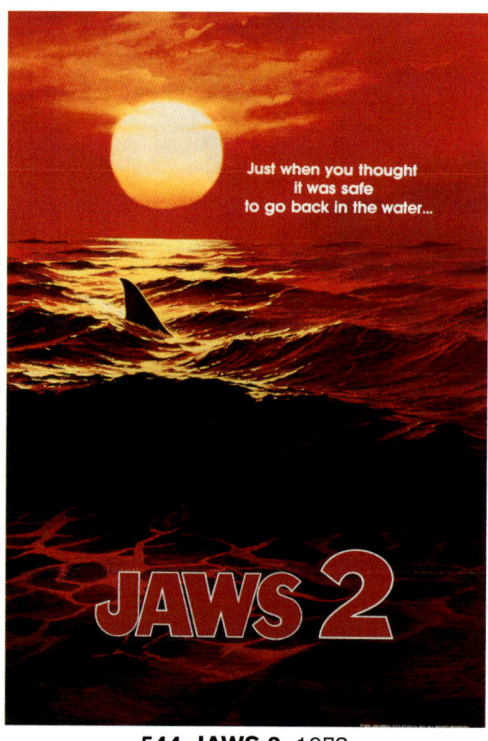
544. JAWS 2, 1978

545. JAWS 2, 1978, Polish

546. BIG WEDNESDAY, 1978

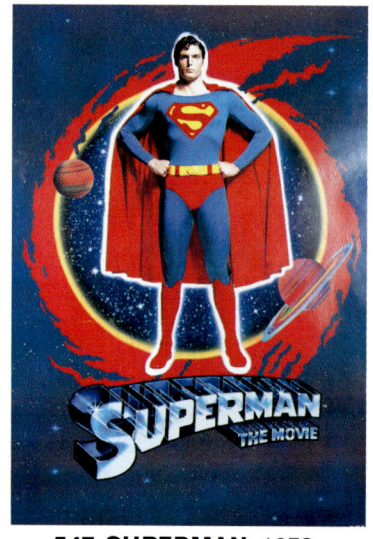
547. SUPERMAN, 1978, Scottish

548. SUPERMAN, 1978, special foil poster

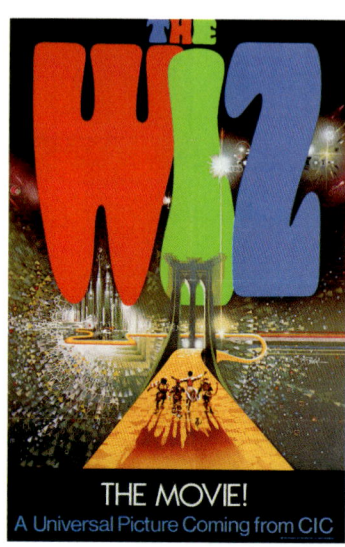
549. THE WIZ, 1978

550. GRAND PRIX, 1967, subway poster

551. STAR WARS, 1977, Russian

552. RUNNING FENCE, 1978, special poster

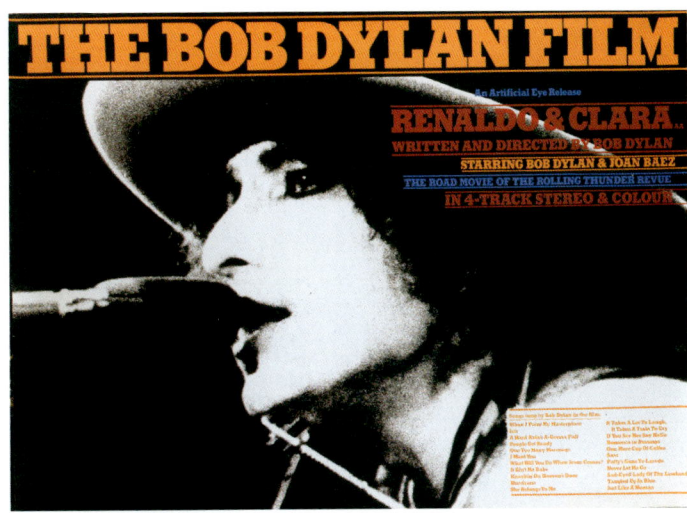
553. RENALDO AND CLARA, 1978, British quad

554. THE TERMINATOR, 1984, British quad

555. SACRIFICE, 1986, Russian

556. RESERVOIR DOGS, 1992, British quad

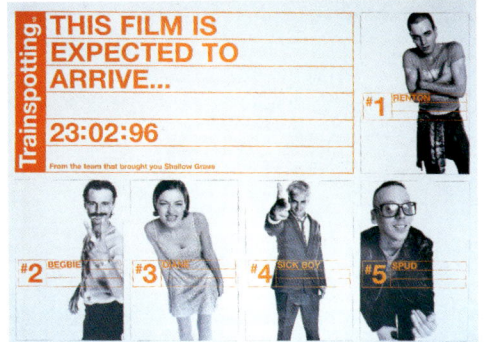
557. TRAINSPOTTING, 1996, British quad

558. TRAINSPOTTING, 1996, British quad

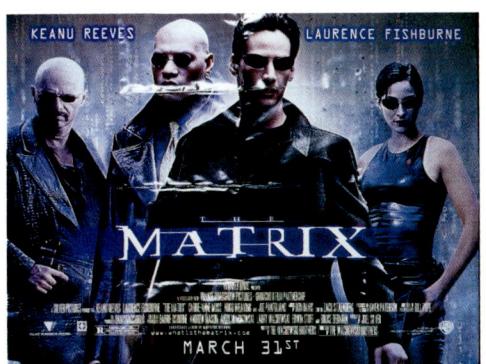
559. THE MATRIX, 1999, subway poster

560. APOCALYPSE NOW, 1979, German

561. 1941, 1979

562. USED CARS, 1980, 2 door panels

563. KAGEMUSHA, 1980, Japanese

564. ALTERED STATES, 1980

565. AN AMERICAN WEREWOLF IN LONDON, 1981

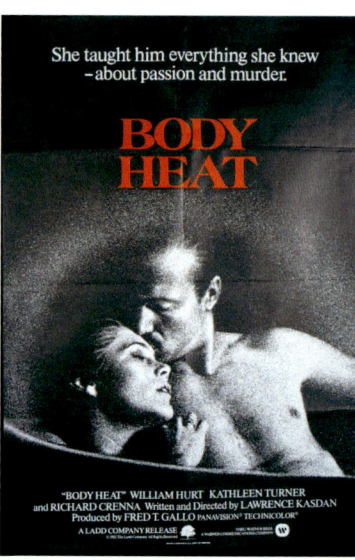
566. BODY HEAT, 1981, English one-sheet

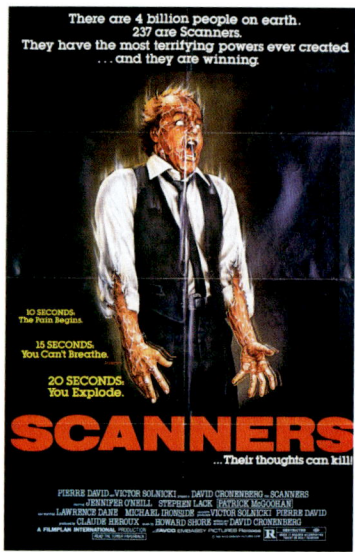
567. SCANNERS, 1981

568. FOR YOUR EYES ONLY, 1981, Japanese

569. FAST TIMES AT RIDGEMONT HIGH, 1982

570. BLADE RUNNER, 1982, special poster

571. POLTERGEIST, 1982

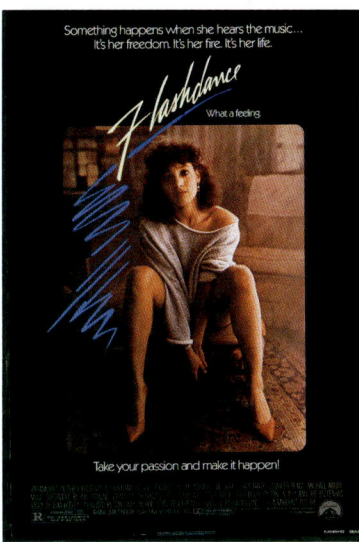
572. FLASHDANCE, 1983

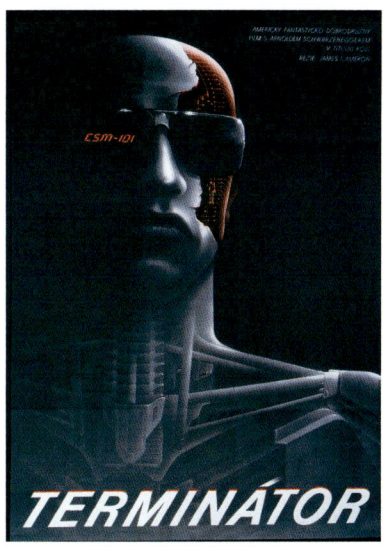
573. THE TERMINATOR, 1984, Czech

574. BACK TO THE FUTURE, 1985

575. THE BREAKFAST CLUB, 1985

576. TROUBLE IN MIND, 1985

577. DOWN BY LAW, 1986

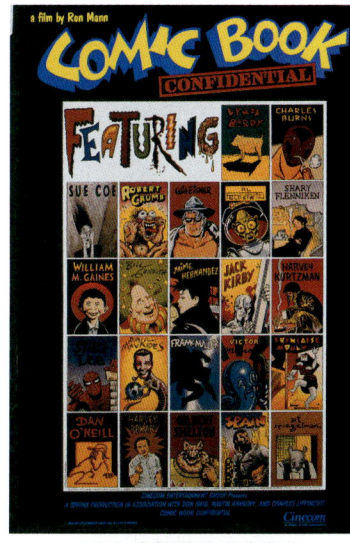
578. COMIC BOOK CONFIDENTIAL, 1988

579. THE LIVING DAYLIGHTS, 1987, Japanese

580. WHO FRAMED ROGER RABBIT, 1988

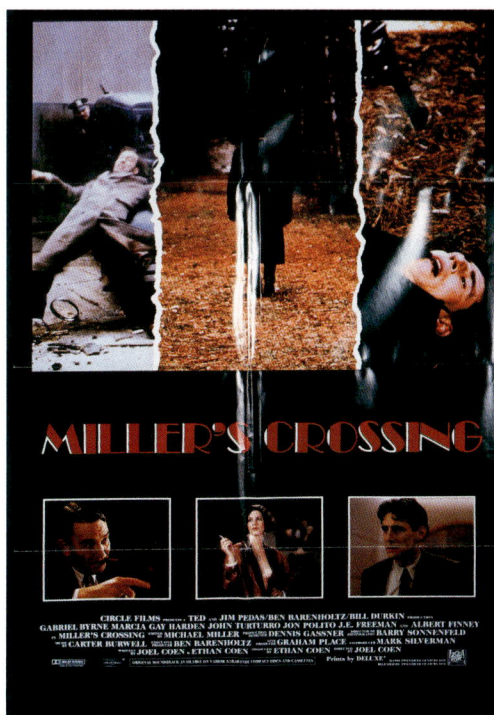
581. MILLER'S CROSSING, 1989

582. POISON, 1991

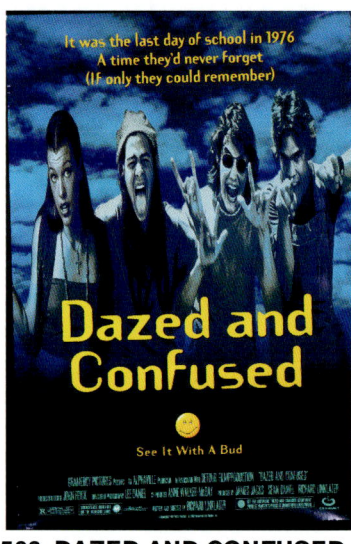
583. DAZED AND CONFUSED, 1993

584. CLERKS, 1994

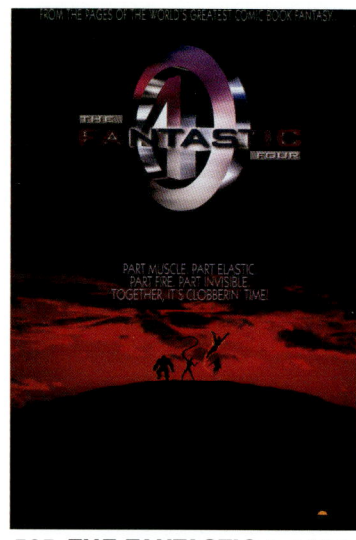
585. THE FANTASTIC 4, 1994

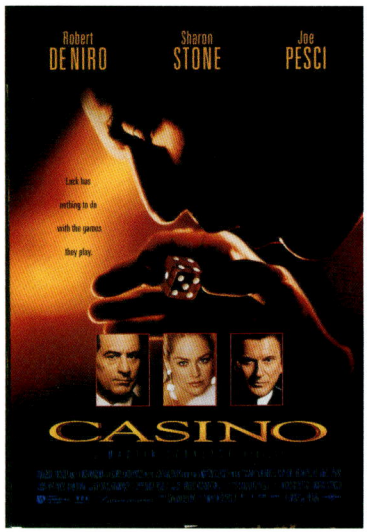
586. CASINO, 1995

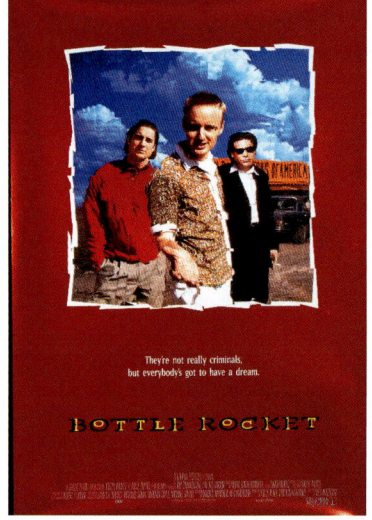
587. BOTTLE ROCKET, 1996

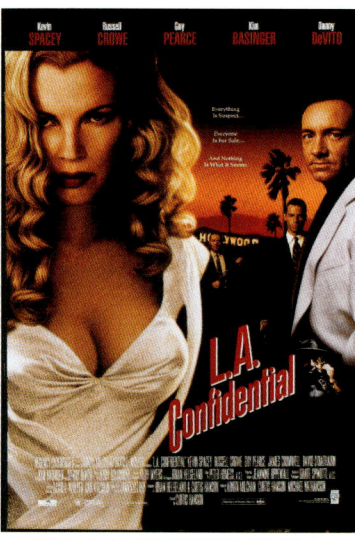
588. L.A. CONFIDENTIAL, 1997

589. THE BRANDON TEENA STORY, 1998

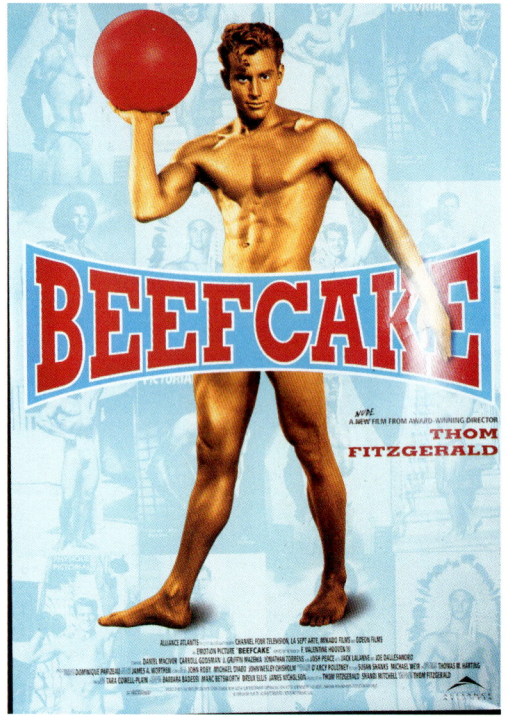
590. BEEFCAKE, 1999

591. GRASS, 1999

592. SECRETARY, 2002

Vintage Hollywood Posters VII Index

1941 561
20,000 Leagues Under The Sea 69
Abbott And Costello Go To Mars . . . 100
Abbott And Costello Meet
Frankenstein 97,99
A.K.A. Cassius Clay 508
Alice Adams 218
Alphaville 480
Altered States 564
An American In Paris 436
An American Werewolf In London . . . 565
Angels With Dirty Faces 205
Animal Crackers 162
Annie Oakley 48
Another New Popeye Comedy 54
The Ape 121
Apocalypse Now 560
Around The World In 80 Minutes 143
Arrowsmith 144
Asphalt Jungle 432
The Astounding She Monster 396
At The Circus 166
Attack Of The 50 Ft. Woman 398
Attack Of The Crab
Monsters 328-332,404
Attack Of The Giant Leeches 306
Back To The Future 574
The Bank Dick 160
Bar 20 Justice 32
Batman 483
The Battleship Potemkin 6
The Beast From Haunted Cave/The
Wasp Woman 374
The Beast With 1,000,000
Eyes 264-271
Beauty And The Beast 67,68
Beefcake 590
Ben-Hur 462
The Bicycle Thief 415
The Big Clock 65
The Big Store 168
Big Wednesday 546
The Black Camel 182
The Black Cat 122
The Black Cat 112
Black Friday 120
Black Orpheus 465
The Black Sleep 393
Blade Runner 570
The Blob 361-369
Block-Heads 175
Blood Feast 472
Blood Of Dracula 281

Bluebeard's 8Th Wife 37
Bob Le Flambeur 416
Body Heat 566
Bolero 30
Bottle Rocket 587
The Brain That Wouldn't Die 349
The Brandon Teena Story 589
Break Of Hearts 217
Breaker Morant 423
Breakfast At Tiffany's 468
The Breakfast Club 575
The Bride Of Frankenstein 92,101
Bride Of The Monster 370
The Bride Wore Black 422
Bright Eyes 124
Bring Me The Head Of Alfredo
Garcia 529
Bringing Up Baby 219
Buck Privates 169
The Bullfighters 180
Bullitt 495-497
Cabaret 517
Captain January 129
Carefree 200
Careless Lady 236
Casablanca 55-57
Casino 586
Cat-Women Of The Moon 242
Charlie Chan At Monte Carlo 191
Charlie Chan At The Olympics 192
Charlie Chan At The Opera 189
Charlie Chan At The Race Track . . . 188
Charlie Chan At The Wax Museum . . . 17
Charlie Chan Carries On 181
Charlie Chan In Egypt 184
Charlie Chan In Honolulu 193
Charlie Chan In London 185
Charlie Chan In Paris 16,187
Charlie Chan In Reno 194
Charlie Chan In Shanghai 18,186
Charlie Chan On Broadway 190
Charlie Chan's Greatest Case 183
A Chump At Oxford 179
City Lights 154
Cleopatra 131
Clerks 584
The Cocoanuts 161
The Colossus Of New York 376-383
Come And See 425
Comic Book Confidential 578
Cool And The Crazy 448
Cool Hand Luke 490
The Crawling Eye 293

Creature From The Black
Lagoon 371,372
The Creature Walks Among Us 405
The Crowd 140
The Crowd Roars 239
Curly Top 127
The Curse Of The Werewolf 351,411,412
Curucu Beast Of The Amazon 262
A Damsel In Distress 35,195
Dark Passage 60
Dark Victory 33
David Copperfield 159
Davy Crockett, King Of The
Wild Frontier 439
A Day At The Races 164
The Day The Earth Stood Still 253
Dazed And Confused 583
Deadly Is The Female 444
The Deadly Mantis 333-340
Death Wish 530
The Deer Hunter 543
Desire 226
Destination Moon 241
The Devil Is A Woman 20
Dirty Harry 511,512
Dodesukaden 505
Dog Day Afternoon 533,534
Donovan's Brain 243
Don't Bother To Knock 430
Double Indemnity 62
Down By Law 577
Downhill Racer 498,499
Dr No 469
Dracula 89,103
Dracula Has Risen From The Grave . 500
Duck Soup 13
Duel 516
Each Dawn I Die 206
Earth Vs The Flying Saucers . . . 272-279
East Is West 2
East Is West 42
Enter The Dragon 521,523
Eraserhead 540
Evelyn Prentice 238
The Exorcist 532
Fahrenheit 451 464
Fanny And Alexander 424
The Fantastic 4 585
Fantastic Voyage 486
Fast Times At Ridgemont High 569
The Fatal Hour 119
Feet First 8
First Men In The Moon 384-391

First Spaceship On Venus 397
A Fistful Of Dollars 488,521
Flash Gordon 72-87
Flashdance 572
The Flying Deuces 177
Fog Over Frisco 230
Footlight Parade 221
For Your Eyes Only 568
Forbidden Planet 283-291
Four's A Crowd 209
Frankenstein 101,202
Frankenstein Meets The Wolf Man . . 88
Frigid Wife 453
From Hell It Came 401
From Russia With Love 478
From The Earth To The Moon 71
The Gay Divorcee 197
The Gay Falcon 58
The General 151
The General Died At Dawn 224
Get Carter 510
The Getaway 518
The Giant Behemoth 402
The Giant Claw 280
Glen Or Glenda 451
Go West 167
The Godson 519
The Gold Rush 9,94
Goldfinger 477
Grand Prix 550
Grass 591
Grease 541,544
The Great Dictator 158
Gulliver's Travels 53
Gun Crazy 426
Gunga Din 208
Hallelujah I'M A Bum 240
A Hard Day's Night 413,479
The Hatchet Man 237
Hearts And Spurs 137
Heidi 130
Hell Divers 225
Hello Dolly 509
Hell's Angels 223
Here Comes The Navy 31
High Noon 438
Hit And Run 135
Hold That Ghost 98
Honor Of The Family 145
Horse Feathers 163
Hot Rod Girl 446
The Hound Of The Baskervilles 231

Vintage Hollywood Posters VII Index

I Married A Monster From Outer Space 395
I Walked With A Zombie 96
I Was A Teenage Frankenstein . 292,317
I Was A Teenage Werewolf 399
Il Boom 419
Illicit 146
Inspiration 147
Invaders From Mars 254-261,263
Invasion Of The Saucer-Men 352-259,373
Invisible Ghost 123
The Invisible Ray 114
The Iron Mask 141
It Came From Outer Space . . . 317,392
It Conquered The World 406
It Happened One Night 211
Jailhouse Rock 440
Jaws 536
Jaws 2 544,547
Jew Suss 45
Juggernaut 93
Kagemusha 563
Kelly's Heroes 506
Kiki 148
The Killing 459
King Kong 111
King Of Burlesque 40
L.A. Confidential 588
La Dolce Vita 417
La Notte 414
The Land Unknown 282,292
Laurel And Hardy 15
Liane Jungle Goddess 447
The Lion In Winter 493
The Little Colonel 126
Little Miss Marker 39
Little Nellie Kelly 213
Little Women 216
The Littlest Rebel 125
The Living Daylights 579
London After Midnight 106
The Lone Rider 12
The Long Goodbye 523,537
Love On The Run 227
Loves Of Pharaoh 134
Macabre 294
Mad Dogs And Englishmen 514
Magnificent Obsession 233
Magnum Force 525-527
A Man And A Woman 487
Man Bait 449
A Man For All Seasons 491

The Man From Planet X 252
Marihuana 49
Mary Poppins 476
Mata Hari 149
The Matrix 559
Men In White 36
Midnight Cowboy 501
Miller's Crossing 581
Minnie 5
Modern Times 155
The Mole People 319-327,403
Monkey Business 14
Monster On The Campus 305
Mr Blandings Builds His Dream House 44
The Mr Wong In Chinatown 118
The Mummy 104
Murders In The Rue Morgue 108
My Little Chickadee 157
My Man Godfrey 222
Mystery Of Mr Wong 115
Niagara 433
Night Of The Demon 341-248
Night Tide 471
North By Northwest 461
Oh You Tony 136
The Old Dark House 109
On Her Majesty's Secret Service . . . 507
One Million Years Bc 481
One Night In The Tropics 235
One, Two, Three 470
Out Of The Past 61
The Outlaw Josey Wales 537,541
Pardon My Sarong 43
Pardon Us 171
Parlor Bedroom And Bath 152
Payment On Demand 455
Persona 463
The Philadelphia Story 220
Pick A Star 174
Pierrot Le Fou 502
Pinky 51
Pinocchio 52,70
A Place In The Sun 429
Plan 9 From Outer Space 360
Planet Of The Apes 494
Poison 582
Poltergeist 571
The Poor Little Rich Girl 128
The Prince And The Showgirl 428
The Producers 492
Psychedelic Sex Kicks 454
Psycho 408-410

Pumping Iron 535
The Raven 350
Rear Window 427,434
Rebecca 232
Rebel Without A Cause 434,488
Red Desert 420
Renaldo And Clara 553
Reservoir Dogs 556
The Return Of The Vampire 90
The Roaring Twenties 207
Robin Hood 520
Rock 'N' Roll Revue 456
A Romance Of Happy Valley 133
Room Service 165
Rose Marie 21-29
Running Fence 552
Saboteur 63
Sacrifice 555
Salesman 503
Sanjuro 418
Saps At Sea 178
Scanners 567
The Scarlet Empress 19
The Sea Hawk 47
Second Chorus 234
Seconds 482
Secretary 592
Seven Days' Leave 142
The Seven Year Itch 445
The Seventh Voyage Of Sinbad . . 70,91
Shaft 513
Shall We Dance 199
She Freak 484
The She-Creature 392,427
Sherlock Holmes Faces Death 59
Sidewalks Of New York 153
Singin' In The Rain 435
Snow White And The Seven Dwarfs 202,282
Son Of Frankenstein 91,92
The Son Of The Sheik 138
Sons Of The Desert 172
Souls In Pawn 452
Sparrows 139
Spartacus 7
The Spy Who Loved Me 539
Star Wars 551
Stocks And Blondes 11
The Story Of Vernon And Irene Castle 196
Strange Cargo 215
The Stranger 64
Sunnyside 132

Sunset Blvd 431
Superman 547,554
Susan Lenox 150
Svengali 107
Sweet Smell Of Success 443
Swing Time 198
Swiss Miss 176
Tarantula 307-216
Tarzan Finds A Son 38
The Terminator 554,557
Test Pilot 210
The Third Man 66
They Learned About Women 34
The Thing That Couldn't Die 304
This Island Earth 295-303
Three Weeks Off 4
Three Wise Girls 228
The Time Machine 466
To Catch A Thief 458
To Kill A Mockingbird 473-475
Tobacco Road 50
Too Hot To Handle 214
Tower Of London 116
The Trail Of The Lonesome Pine 3
Trainspotting 557,9
The Trip 485
Trouble In Mind 576
Umbrellas Of Cherbourg 421
Un Chien Andalou 7
Underwater 450
The Unholy Three 105
Used Cars 562
The Walking Dead 94,522
War Exposition 1
Way Out West 173
Westworld 528
When Worlds Collide 244-251,375
White Christmas 442
The White Cockatoo 46
White Zombie 110
Who Framed Roger Rabbit 580
The Wild Bunch 504
The Wild One 437
Willy Wonka And The Chocolate Factory 515
The Wiz 549
The Wizard Of Oz 201
The Working Man 229
Wuthering Heights 212
You Can't Cheat An Honest Man . . . 156
You'Ll Find Out 170
Young Frankenstein 531
Ziegfeld Follies 41